STO

FRIENDS
OF ACPL

3 1833 00580 6929

D1161506

TO THE ZOO IN A PLASTIC BOX

"John and George Newmark, identical twins, have been addicted to animals since boyhood. Longing to follow in the steps of Cherry Kearton, the British naturalist and photographer, they joined an infantry regiment which had a battalion in India so that they could study the local natural history. Since the war and their return to civilian life they have spent their holidays traveling abroad (to those places the Army never sent them) and collecting animals for the London Zoo. This book describes their adventures and offers some advice to young zoologists. Light, cheery, and unpretentious, it bowls along at a fine pace. Some nice comic drawings by G. A. Gammon and the authors."

The London Times Literary Supplement

The authors arriving at the London Zoo with a collection of reptiles and insects

John & George Newmark

To the Zoo in a Plastic Box

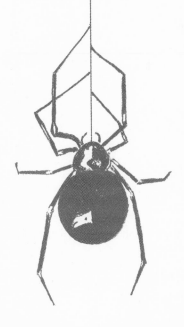

Random House • New York

First published in the United States 1965
© Copyright, 1963, 1965, by John and George Newmark

All rights reserved under International and Pan-American Copyright
Conventions. Published in New York by Random House, Inc., and
in London, England, by Routledge & Kegan Paul Ltd.

Library of Congress Catalog Card Number: 65-10496

Manufactured in the United States of America

1 165

TO *Mother and Father*
WHO STILL PUT UP WITH US

U. S. 1294949

Contents

TO THE ZOO IN A PLASTIC BOX

 Introduction

It should be made clear right from the start that this is not a scientific book on reptiles and insects. There are scores of books written by experts dealing with these animals in a correct and scientific manner, and if the student of zoology wants to study the digestive system of a ladybird, or the distribution of warts on the Warty Toad, he will not find the answers here.

This is a book with a difference; two differences, in fact. First, it deals with the collecting of reptiles and insects for the purpose of presenting them to the London Zoo, or to any other Zoo for that matter. Secondly, it has been written jointly by twins, and identical twins at that.

We have been twins now for fifty years, and during the whole of this period, at frequent and regular intervals, we have been placed together, side by side, horizontally or vertically, for the sole purpose of being compared with one another. Family friends and relations and even complete strangers have studied us at close range and pronounced us to be like two peas in a pod. We have identical likes and dislikes, identical mannerisms, identical voices, and possibly we did look like two peas at a very early age, but peas remain circular in shape. We didn't.

Among other things we are both fond of, animals rank very high indeed. So does the London Zoo, quite naturally. Ever since our pram-riding days we have been frequent visitors to the Zoological Gardens, and even before we went into long trousers we had demonstrated our very real interest in the Zoo by making them a present of one of our pets. It was not until after the Second World War, however, that we became Fellows; and having taken this step, we decided to take an even more active interest and to start collecting, not as a paid job but simply as a hobby. Most people have a hobby of some sort. Some collect stamps, or marble statues, or shrunken heads; others paint, or put ships into bottles, or breed canaries in odd shapes. We collect reptiles and insects for the Zoo. A slightly unusual hobby it is true, but all the more interesting for that.

We are not quite sure why we like doing this. Possibly the reason originates from the knowledge that when we presented a foreign bird to the Zoo many years ago, we gained free admission. Or perhaps it stems from the fact that we cannot keep pets in our flat in Baker Street, and at the same time remain on friendly terms with the landlord; nor with the occupants of the flats above and below who would protest strongly if a pair of Howling Monkeys disturbed their peaceful slumbers at six o'clock every morning. A tropical aquarium sits in a corner of the sitting room, and a pair of wood pigeons from nearby Regent's Park alight on the dining-room window sill to nibble biscuit crumbs, but these can hardly be called pets. By way of compensation we enjoy collecting small creatures and presenting them to the Zoo where we know they will receive first-class treatment in first-class surroundings. It is also rather fun to visit the Zoo and see our birds or reptiles or insects on display, and to be able to nudge one another and say, "That's ours."

So for the past few years we have made a point of spending our holidays abroad, and our choice of countries has depended very largely on two factors: the distribution of animals likely to be found, and the distribution of relations likely to put us up. Because semitropical regions offer more scope for collecting than does France, or Belgium, or Holland, our first collecting-on-holiday trip was to Morocco. We are fortunate in having an unknown number of relations scattered in various parts of the globe, and we propose descending upon them, one by one, year by year, staying with each for two or three weeks, or until there is no food left. We have already taken advantage of one sister in New York State, another one in Florida, and an aunt in New York City. In return for their hospitality we offer to remove any unwanted reptiles and insects from their homes and gardens, selecting those specimens large enough, colorful enough, or uncommon enough for presentation to the Zoo on our return home.

This, then, is our hobby, and for the benefit of

anyone with similar interests we have given some prac-
tical instructions in the art of collecting, and described
some of our own experiences in this book. We hope to
continue collecting until our ninetieth birthday which
we shall celebrate by presenting each other to the Zoo.

1:  How It All Began

It all began when we were about five. At that pink and delicate age of innocence, we lived in a large house in Hampstead, with about an acre of garden—the pride and joy of our parents (the garden, not us). In one corner of the garden was a greenhouse, and in the greenhouse were a number of glass-covered seed boxes full of annuals in various stages of growth. These seed boxes were the special responsibility of William, the gardener, who cherished and tended them with loving devotion. He visited them daily, even on his day off, to see what progress the young plants had made, and to water them and generally ensure that all was well with every single one.

We, too, cherished the seed boxes, but for a vastly different reason. We were not in the least bit interested in their contents; after all, who, at the age of five, wants to wait weeks or months while tiny little seeds grow into flowers? There were already plenty of flowers in the garden anyway. We wanted something that moved, something that we could watch. And the seed boxes, without their present contents, would be ideal for our own vile and secret purpose. Accordingly, one Sunday afternoon when William was busy elsewhere, we crept into the greenhouse, selected one of the seed boxes and, between us, carried it down to the bottom of the garden where, behind the safety of a hedge, we tipped the contents onto a rubbish heap. This accomplished, we returned to the greenhouse and repeated the deed with a second box, and then with a third. Finally, when we had gained possession of three empty seed boxes, we hauled them off to our own corner of the garden.

Perhaps it should here be explained that each member of our fairly considerable family had his or her own corner of the garden. Our four elder sisters each had fairly extensive sections and grew a profusion of colorful plants. Edward, our elder brother, also had quite a large portion of ground and grew shrubs as well as flowers. We, the youngest, had the smallest patch and the least in it, if weeds are excluded. Sometimes, when nobody else was around, we would pick some choice blossoms from the other gardens and stick them into our own bare patch. And so it was, on this Sunday afternoon, that we found ourselves in possession of three empty seed boxes and an almost empty patch of garden.

We placed the seed boxes on the pathway at the edge of our patch, furnished them with one or two suitable stones and pieces of rock, and then proceeded on our very first collecting trip, equipped with a seaside spade, a bucket, and William's cloth cap. The cap, it should be added, made an admirable butterfly net if used with a little skill. Our destination was again the rubbish heap where, in the hidden depths, William had often shown us all sorts of insects. Without so much as a glance at the young plants which now lay scattered and forlorn on the heap of rubbish, we dived down into the depths. Within half an hour, all three seed boxes had occupants. The first one became the Insect House and contained several wood lice and some ants; the second box became the Reptile House and was inhabited by a slug and two worms, both of which wriggled uncomfortably on the bare wood, feeling very much in the nude. And the third and final box became our Butterfly House, wherein dwelt one very tattered Cabbage White which we had caught in William's cap.

Thus opened London's newest, smallest and most unsuccessful Zoo. Naturally, we considered it to be a branch of the London Zoo—an overflow, so to speak; and, with complete disregard for the regulations governing the price of admission to that establishment, we decided on our own scale of charges: a penny for grownups, and half price for children under three. Since we ourselves were five, this placed us in the category of grownups which, we felt, was necessary since we owned the zoo. All that was required now was the co-operation of the general public.

We stood hopefully by the front door waiting for the stream of customers to seek admission. Plenty of people walked by, one or two even spoke to us or simply said, "Hello, twins," and walked on; but nobody walked in. After about twenty minutes, we began to ask ourselves why no one had shown any apparent desire to visit our zoo; we thought perhaps we both ought to have had a wash first. We looked at each other and confirmed that this was indeed the case, but it was now too late to do anything about it. And then, quite suddenly, it occurred to us that none of the people passing by even knew that a zoo existed in our garden, since we hadn't told anybody about it, nor had we thought of putting up a notice. In any case, we had no materials with which to make a notice; William would no doubt make one for us the next day.

Meanwhile, the general public would have to wait to see our zoo, but there was no reason why our own family shouldn't have a preview. We went back into the house and told our four sisters that they could visit our zoo, provided they each paid a penny. They did so somewhat fearfully, knowing that the alternative might be painful. So did the maid and so did the cook, aware of the untold damage we were capable of doing in their respective departments. Our collection of animals had, so far, cost us nothing apart from a good deal of energy and a torn pair of socks; so every penny that we were able to extract from members of the family would be pure profit. To be quite fair, we did discuss the possibility of spending our profit on food for the animals, but finally spent it on sweets for ourselves.

The zoo's history was brief. To begin with, most of the creatures disappeared through cracks in the seed boxes; the wood lice and the worms departed downwards into the earth; the slug simply oozed its way through a space between the top of the box and the glass lid; and the butterfly expired in a corner. And finally, there was William. He had learned from the maid and it was confirmed by the cook, that three wooden boxes, looking suspiciously like three of his precious seed boxes, had been turned into Reptile, Insect and Butterfly Houses and were now on display by the side of our patch at the distant end of the garden. Naturally enough, William went to see for himself. We did not understand a good deal of what he said because most of it appeared to be in a foreign language, but very shortly afterwards we were both removed from the scene by the scruff of our dirty necks and sent to bed, supperless.

2: A Present for the Zoo

We made our first presentation to the London Zoo at the age of eight. We gave them a tortoise. It was a very ordinary tortoise which had originally been given to us as a birthday present by our Aunt Toosie. Knowing our fondness for anything in the animal line, she had decided that a tortoise would keep us out of mischief for several weeks. Our opinion of aunts rose to a fairly high level and in honor of this particular one who had so thoughtfully given us the tortoise, we named it after her. Toosie the tortoise lived very happily in the garden during the summer holidays, thriving on dandelions, vegetables, and apple cores. But toward the end of the holidays when we had to consider the gloomy prospects of returning to boarding school, the inevitable question arose: Who would look after Toosie? We wondered whether William would oblige, but we were not on the best of terms with him. The painful incident concerning the seed boxes had

never been completely forgotten; furthermore, he had warned us what he proposed to do with the tortoise if he ever discovered it wandering about in the vicinity of his precious vegetable garden. So we rejected William. What about Edward, our elder brother? No; out of the question. Edward was rather interested in biology, and any unlucky toad or newt that came his way quickly found itself in a killing bottle. It was altogether too risky to entrust him with Toosie who would undoubtedly have finished up in various bottles, all neatly labeled. Perhaps one of our sisters would undertake the job of looking after her? But they also had to be ruled out; they were all far too occupied with such dull things as needlework, dancing lessons, and cooking. One of them even sang.

After considering the problem at some length, we came to the conclusion that there was only one thing to do; rather a pleasant thing, in fact, and the more we thought about it, the more we decided that it was quite definitely the thing to do: present Toosie to the Zoo. We had been to the Zoo several times during the school holidays, and had paid a lot of attention to the labels on the cages. For some reason these labels held a mild fascination for us, though there was nothing very extraordinary about them. They merely indicated the names of the animals displayed, where they came from, and who presented them. For example: Java Sparrow, *Padda oryzivora*. Java, Sumatra, and southeast Asia. Presented by Mr. Tomkinson. How wonderful our names would look on one of those labels! Think of it: Tortoise. Africa. Presented by John and George. Or should it be Master J. and G. Newmark? No, we preferred just plain John and George since that was how we were known at home. Nobody ever called us Master Newmark except unimportant people such as the teachers at school. John and George it would be, and we would give instructions to that effect.

The fanciful thoughts and imaginations of eight-year-olds know no bounds. We were going straight to the top. We would approach only the very highest officials, and be received at the Main Entrance to the Zoo by the Director of the Zoo. After a short speech of welcome—we were not quite sure whether we would have to make the speech, or whether the Director would—the moment would come for us to present him with Toosie amid cheers and clapping from the crowd assembled for the occasion, and the clicking of news reporters' cameras. Our pictures would appear in every newspaper in the land, and all the news reels in all the cinemas would record the event. In no time at all we would be invited to the Palace to become Sir John and Sir George. Our names would go down in history.

Pleasant thoughts. Most thoughts tend to be pleasant

at the age of eight. No one of that age ever thinks about income tax, or the latest increase in fares, or even about Monday morning. Our own thoughts were generally centered around animals and birds and small creatures, and we were in constant trouble at school for daydreaming and inattention in class. While the rest of the class would be delving into the mysteries of algebra, or trying to sort out how many gills and pints went into a peck or a bushel, we would be quietly discussing the nesting habits of the turtledove. Not even the headmaster could tell us very much about the turtledove. We told him. Our end-of-term reports were remarkable for the variety of ways our form-master found for saying the same thing about different subjects. History: inattention throughout the term has resulted in deplorable marks. Geography: complete lack of interest has produced lamentable results. Arithmetic: would do considerably better if even a spark of interest or a brief moment of attention was given to the subject. French: shows an interest in everything except French. Perhaps the prize remark was the one which read, alongside the heading, Scripture: Let us pray. If one of us failed to come bottom of the class at the end of the term, it was only because the other one had managed to do so. The headmaster and his staff were unanimous in their choice of suitable nicknames for us; we were openly known as Abomination and Desolation.

To return to the tortoise. We had agreed that we would present her to the Zoo, and a few days before the end of the holidays we duly arrived at the main entrance carrying Toosie carefully in the bottom of a bucket. She lay there comfortably on a bed of potato peels, poking her head in and out of her shell and displaying a certain amount of curiosity at her unusual surroundings. We wore our Sunday suits for the occasion, even though it was Monday. Monday was half-price day at the Zoo, the day that most of our visits took place. This particular Monday we felt important, very important indeed, as we handed over our entrance money at the turnstile and entered the Zoo. True, we had forgotten to inform the Director of our intention to present him with a tortoise, so we were not particularly surprised to find he was not there to greet us. However, we made our way through the crowds, no doubt looking a trifle odd carrying a bucket between us, for several people turned and stared at us, while some peered right into the bucket and beheld Toosie. This pleased us. Toosie was being admired, and would surely become the center of attraction, the showpiece of the entire Zoo.

In due course we—and Toosie—reached our destination, the Reptile House, which in those days stood where the present Bird House now stands. Near the entrance was a large open-air enclosure in which roamed a number of tortoises, plodding about in their slow and determined manner. Some of them were very much larger than Toosie, but others were about her shape and size, and there was no doubt at all that she would quickly make new friends without the slightest difficulty. It was quite obvious that the Zoo went in for tortoises, and the authorities would certainly be delighted to have another one to add to their collection.

A low railing round the enclosure supported a number of labels. These were of considerable interest to us, and we examined them critically. They were a nice size, yes, and in a prominent position too. Visitors to the Reptile House couldn't help but notice them, and OUR label would be among them, right in the very center.

We entered the building. The Head Keeper was inside, talking to one of the visitors. We put the bucket gently down so that other visitors would be able to see inside, and waited. Soon the Head Keeper saw us waiting there, and sensing that something important was about to happen, he came forward to meet us. We straightened our ties.

"We would very much like to present you with a tortoise," we told him in a manner loud enough to be heard right across the Zoo. With those carefully selected words, we handed over Toosie in the bucket and waited expectantly for an address of thanks. We also wondered with a tinge of anxiety whether the Head Keeper in accepting the tortoise would remember to give us back the bucket.

He did. He not only gave us back the bucket, but he gave us back Toosie as well. He never even lifted her out, but left her sitting there on the potato peels. He had glanced into the bucket and must surely have seen her sitting in the bottom, but nevertheless he handed her back to us. He was very nice about it and thanked us most earnestly for our very kind and generous offer, but unfortunately he was unable to accept it. He went on to explain that there were already no less than twenty-eight tortoises in the outside enclosure, and several others dispersed in various cages inside, and it was impossible to accept any more. There just wasn't room.

We were profoundly dismayed. We had offered the Zoo an extremely rare creature—at least, it was rare to us—and they were unable to accept it because they had no room. It was a major disaster, and we were bitterly disappointed.

The Head Keeper returned to continue his duties, and we slowly walked out of the building, carrying the bucket between us. Poor Toosie. She looked a little sad now with her head and feet tucked away in her shell. And poor us. We were sad, too, but consoled ourselves with the fact that we had at least offered her to the Zoo. It was no fault of ours that she was not wanted.

We stopped again at the enclosure outside containing the twenty-eight tortoises, and examined the labels once more. Perhaps they were not quite in the best position after all; possibly a shade too high, and perhaps there were too many of them. Our label might not have been noticed among so many others. No, it was not an ideal place after all.

An idea occurred to us. Why not present Toosie anyway? They already had twenty-eight tortoises, so why not make it twenty-nine? One more wouldn't make any difference, and Toosie would be simply thrilled at having so many friends. There was hardly anyone about. Nobody would see us, and nobody would know. We stood close by the railing. One of us bent down, lifted Toosie from the bucket, reached over the railing, and deposited her gently on the grass.

The deed was done; we headed rapidly toward the nearest exit. It was a pity that no label would appear on that enclosure, announcing to the world at large that John and George had presented the Zoo with a tortoise. Our rise to fame was not to be. Our pictures would not be published in the newspapers, not even on the women's page. Nor would we receive the expected summons to Buckingham Palace. We sincerely hoped we would not receive a summons from the police. But as we passed through the turnstiles and left the Zoo behind us, we began to feel rather pleased. True, things had not gone quite the way we had planned, but the most important part had been successfully accomplished.

We had presented the Zoo with a tortoise.

3: A Tip for the Director

Not long after the presentation of our tortoise, we had another occasion to visit the Zoo. This time it was all about a goldfish. We had acquired it from a pet shop, and had paid the considerable sum of fourpence for it—the equivalent in those days of two bars of chocolate. It lived in a small aquarium on the window sill in the sitting room, and behaved in much the same way as any other goldfish. Over a period of time, however, it grew rather a long tail; not an ordinary fishy sort of tail like a sardine's, but a long drooping affair which hung down and trailed behind it like a flimsy curtain. This surely could not be an ordinary fourpenny goldfish, not with a tail like that; it must be something extremely rare and valuable, and it was imperative that we should do something about it. We went into conference. Two alternatives were worth considering: first the pet shop from which we had bought the fish. Perhaps the man who had sold it to us would know why it was growing a special tail. But the more we thought about it, the more we disliked the idea of asking him. He might want to take it back and give us an ordinary one in exchange. No, it was altogether too risky to approach him on the matter. The other alternative was to go and see the fishmonger on High Street. His shop was always full of strange and exotic-looking fish, so perhaps he would be able to enlighten us. But in the end we had to rule him out too; it was Thursday, and Thursday was early-closing day.

"Let's take it to the Zoo," one of us suggested, "and show it to Mr. Boulenger." That was a brilliant suggestion. Mr. Boulenger was the Director of the Aquarium at the Zoo. He knew absolutely everything there was to be known about fish, and he had written several books about them. In fact we had been given one of his books for a Christmas present. There was certainly nobody better qualified to tell us whether our goldfish was an ordinary one or a special one. Mr. Boulenger

was our man, and to him we would go that very day.

On went our Sunday suits once again as we prepared ourselves for yet another important mission. The gold-fish was caught and transferred from the aquarium into a jam jar, and after making sure that we looked reasonably well washed, we set off for the Zoo. On arrival we paid for our admission, and as we did so, we again felt that sense of pride and importance, and held the jam jar in a prominent position for everyone to see. After all, we were not just ordinary people out to spend a day at the Zoo. We were important, and had an important man to meet.

The Aquarium was opposite the main gate, under the Mappin Terraces. It had been opened not so long ago by His Majesty King George V, and was considered to be the finest aquarium in the world. As we walked smartly up the steps and into the entrance hall, a keeper noticed our jam jar containing the precious goldfish.

"That's a nice-looking fish you've got there," he remarked.

"Yes," we replied. That was a good start anyway.

"Where are you taking it?" asked the keeper.

"We want to show it to Mr. Boulenger," one of us answered. "You see, it has a very unusual tail for a goldfish, and we think it might be a very rare one."

The keeper examined it for several moments and agreed that it was indeed an unusual specimen. That was most encouraging.

"Have you an appointment with Mr. Boulenger?" he asked us with a tinge of doubt in his voice.

"Oh yes," we told him. As far as we were concerned, we did have an appointment with Mr. Boulenger. It never entered our heads that Mr. Boulenger might not have an appointment to see us. Nor did it occur to us that Mr. Boulenger might never have heard of us, nor been aware of our existence. After all, we were only eight.

The keeper, however, was evidently satisfied that we had an appointment, for he directed us to a door marked Private. He knocked; a voice from within called, "Come in," and in we went. The door closed behind us. We were in the presence of the mighty. There we stood jam jar in hand, not quite knowing how to begin, nor even how to address a person of such importance. Mr. Boulenger sat at a huge desk in the center of the room. A large aquarium rested on a table in a corner, and we made a mental note to remove our own aquarium at home from the window sill and place it on a table in a corner. Bookshelves lined all four walls, and most of the volumes appeared to be about fish. We would certainly have to buy a few more fishy books for our room. On the desk was a curious ash tray shaped like a fish.

It is possible that we would have stood there for a fortnight if the Great Man had not broken the spell.

"Good afternoon," he said, smiling.

"Good afternoon," we replied in harmony. There was a·pause. Each of us was hoping the other one would begin.

"Have you come to see me about anything in particular?" he inquired, glancing at the jam jar.

"Oh yes," we suddenly remembered. "Can you tell us what sort of fish this is?"

We held up our jam jar. The goldfish looked magnificent, obviously at its very best. Its long drooping tail swayed gracefully, almost touching the bottom of the jar.

The Great Man took the jar from our trembling hands and proceeded to examine it. Holding it against the light, he turned it slowly around two or three times. We made another mental note; next time we bought a fish from a pet shop, we would hold it against the light and examine it before actually paying for it. It was the correct way to tell whether it was—well, whether it was—anyway, it was the correct thing to do. Mr. Boulenger had just done it, so it must be right.

"Yes," said the Great Man, handing the jam jar back to us, "you have a very fine specimen of the Fan-tailed Goldfish. *Carassius auratus,*" he added, with a note of finality.

We nodded in agreement. In future, when we wanted to buy a goldfish, we would not simply ask for a goldfish; we would ask for a *Carassius auratus.*

"It cost fourpence," we told him. "Do you think it is worth any more? Ninepence, perhaps, or even a shilling?"

"Yes, indeed," Mr. Boulenger replied. "I would say it is probably worth more than that; four or five shillings would be nearer the mark."

We were jubilant. Our fish was a *Carassius auratus,* it was a very valuable specimen, and we had spoken to the Director of the Aquarium.

"Thank you very much, thank you very much indeed," we said politely, knowing that our interview was coming to an end and wondering how we could prolong it. But there was nothing else left to say. We picked up the jam jar containing our precious *Carassius auratus* and began to move toward the door. Suddenly we remembered our Mother's advice: Always leave a tip for the keepers at the Zoo, and with anyone else who helped us in any way. One of us dug a hand into a pocket and produced a sixpenny bit. Solemnly it was laid on the desk in front of the Director.

Our faces were identical shades of crimson as we left the office, prouder than we had ever been before.

4: Military Operations

The years passed by, as is their custom, and we grew from small boys to big boys. Our interest in anything relating to natural history also grew, and at school we invariably came top in natural history subjects, bottom in everything else. From day school to boarding school, then on to public school, our end-of-term reports made sad reading, brightened only by the brief but praiseworthy remarks in the column marked Natural History, which we were quick to point out to anyone who happened to look at the reports, hoping they wouldn't read the remainder.

During our childhood days, we had read every Cherry Kearton book available; Cherry Kearton, the naturalist and photographer, was our hero, and we longed to visit the places he had been to, notably the Mountains of the Moon, in East Africa. Films—the old, silent variety—had been made of some of his travels and the local cinema could always be sure of at least two visits by us whenever a Cherry Kearton film was showing. Africa, India, South America, in fact any part of the world that was tropical and jungly, had a magic spell for us, but the big problem was, how were we to get there? Where was the money coming from?

By the time we left school, the problem was no nearer solution, though our urge to go was just as great. It seemed that there was only one thing to do: save up. We would save every single penny of our pocket money; we would give up sweets completely; and we'd walk everywhere instead of going by bus. At Christmas, and for our birthday, we would simply ask outright for money. We had plenty of uncles and aunts as well as our own immediate family, and if they all became generous and dug down deep enough into their pockets, it wouldn't be long before we had enough for the fare to Africa. Alas! Christmas came and went, so did our birthday, and when we came to add up our grand total we barely had enough to get us as far as Margate. So we spent the lot on sweets.

Then, one miserable cloudy day when we were in the vicinity of Camden Town, quite near the Zoo, it began to rain heavily. We took shelter in the nearest doorway, which happened to be the entrance to an Army recruiting office. Our eyes alighted simultaneously on a notice pinned to the wall: JOIN THE ARMY AND SEE THE WORLD. We looked at one another, each aware that the same idea had flashed through our minds. Join the Army and go to Africa! Join the Army and go to India! Join the Army and go anywhere we liked! What did we need money for? All we had to do was join the Army and we would be paid for going. In other words, our problem was solved. Money was no longer an obstacle. But Mother might be.

Our spirits rose to new heights as we took the next bus home to discuss the idea of an army career with the rest of the family. It didn't matter to us very much whether we joined the Royal Signals, or the Infantry, or the Artillery, or any other branch of the Army. Our sole aim was simply to go abroad and see something of the animal life in the tropics. All we had to do was to choose a regiment which was stationed in a tropical country; either Africa or India would do very nicely.

That evening, after supper, we brought up the subject of joining the Army. Rather nervously, when the family was assembled in the sitting room, we painted a glowing picture of life in the Army, particularly after we had reached the rank of Major, which we could easily do within a year or so. We pictured ourselves in command of a battalion, keeping law and order in one of the far-flung outposts of the Empire. We saw ourselves quelling a riot in Poona, then being rapidly transferred to deal with a dangerous situation which existed on the North West Frontier. Mother listened attentively, and occasionally uttered "Yes, dear" or "Really, dear?" between marshmallows. Father lit a cigarette, sank into the deepest chair and pondered in silence. We sought encouragement from Edward, our elder brother. Edward's opinion in family matters was generally considered sound and sensible; he was two years older than we, and had done extremely well at school, coming top in all the subjects in which we came bottom. Edward, much to our surprise, was on our side and thought it a very good idea for us to join the Army. Whereupon three of our four sisters promptly agreed with him; the fourth, Dorothy, was in America, and therefore not even aware of our intentions. "It would be rather nice to have a couple of Generals in the family," mused Sylvia, idly turning over the pages of *The Tatler*. Mother finally agreed on the grounds that we could always resign if we didn't like it. Father agreed too, because Mother did; besides, he wanted to read the *Evening Standard* without further interruption.

The next day, we returned to the Army recruiting office and let it be known to the Sergeant-in-charge that the British Army was about to be reinforced by two young men who wished to go abroad at the first opportunity. "In which case," said the Sergeant-in-charge, "all you have to do is to join an Infantry Regiment; they nearly all have a battalion stationed abroad, mostly India." He produced a list of the regiments, showing where the battalions were stationed. We looked down the list and came to The Queen's Own Royal West Kent Regiment, 2nd Battalion, Aldershot. 1st Battalion, Trimulgherry, India.

"This one will do fine," one of us exclaimed. "Trimulgherry sounds very tropical."

"Good tiger country," added the Sergeant-in-charge, as if aware of our prime reason for wishing to enlist. Those three words settled it. We handed the list back.

"May I have your names, please," asked the Sergeant, sitting down behind a desk. "I take it you both want to join together?" As a matter of fact, we had previously decided that only one of us—George—

would join to start with; John could join later on if
George wrote to say that Army life was likely to agree
with us.

And so it was that we became separated for a period;
John went back home, while George was sent to the
Regimental Depot at Maidstone, where he donned the
uniform of the British Army and became Number
6342645, Recruit G. Newmark—mainly because a sergeant in Camden Town had casually mentioned that
Trimulgherry was "good tiger country."

George spent several months at Maidstone, learning
the art of soldiering. He also made preliminary
inquiries regarding the possibility of being transferred
to the other battalion at Trimulgherry, and learned
that all one had to do was apply for a transfer as soon
as one's training was completed. So, out of working
hours—and, for that matter, during working hours—
he read up all his books on Indian birds, reptiles and
insects with renewed enthusiasm.

In due course, when his training was finished,
George was posted to Aldershot where the 2nd Battalion was stationed. And exactly a week later, John
enlisted as planned and arrived at the entrance to the
Regimental Depot at Maidstone. It should here be
explained that in those days soldiers were not permitted to wear civilian clothes unless they had served
a period of two years; until that time they were
required to wear uniforms, and it was in uniform that
George had stepped smartly out of the Depot gates on
his way to Aldershot. And a week later, John turned
up at the gates in civilian clothes. As he walked in
through the gates, a military policeman on duty
stopped him.

"Hullo, Newmark, what are you doing back here? You were posted to Aldershot last week, weren't you?"

John realized at once that the policeman had mistaken him for George; but before he could explain things, the policeman fired another question at him in menacing tones. "And why are you wearing civilian clothes?"

"Young man," John began, with the air of one who is about to score a point, "do you expect me to come here with nothing on?"

"Consider yourself a soldier under open arrest!" barked the policeman, scarlet with fury.

"I'll consider it," replied John.

The policeman turned purple. "Make it close arrest!" he shouted, advancing toward John to escort him to the guardroom.

At this highly inflammable moment, the Adjutant came over from the nearby Officers' Mess. The Adjutant was responsible for meeting new recruits and ensuring that they were officially welcomed, and fitted out with uniform, kit and equipment.

"Ah, you've arrived already; I wasn't expecting you for another hour or so." He shook hands with John and looked him up and down. "My goodness," he exclaimed in astonished tones, "you look exactly like your brother who left last week! Are you twins by any chance?"

"Yes, sir, we are," John replied. He paused, trying to think of something else to say. "We've been twins— er—quite some time." He cast a sideways glance at the policeman who was beginning to express acute embarrassment. "Lots of people mistake us for one another," John added with a twinkle.

The policeman retired, unaware that he was merely the first of a long string of military gentlemen who were to be confused and confounded by our resemblance to each other.

Six months later we were reunited at Aldershot, and it was possible to discuss the prospects of joining the 1st Battalion in India. We had already put our names down as volunteers to go, and now it was only a question of waiting. In the meantime we drilled, went on route marches, polished our boots, cleaned our rifles, and stood on guard, all for the regal sum of fourteen shillings a week. Some of this went on more books about the natural history of India; the rest went on cakes and cups of tea.

Being twins, and being in the same regiment, we were something of a military nuisance, especially to the Provost Sergeant, poor soul. He never quite knew which of us was which, and he never gave up trying to convince us that he did. One of the favorite punishments given by the officers was "seven days C.B." This meant that the culprit was confined to barracks for seven days, and it was the usual punishment given for minor crimes such as being late on parade, having dirty buttons or a rusty rifle. The soldier so punished would then find himself performing all sorts of tiresome and distasteful tasks during the next seven days, generally under the watchful and critical eye of the Provost Sergeant or one of his military policemen. The chores selected included such jobs as peeling potatoes for several hundred troops, or doing the washing up, or scrubbing miles of drains and gutters. If there was nothing better to do, the kitchen could always be relied upon to supply a dozen greasy buckets for polishing, which

the Provost Sergeant would hand around to those unfor-
tunate enough to be doing "seven days." "And I want
'em to shine until I can see my face in 'em," he would
add, ruthlessly. No one ever had sufficient courage to
ask him why he wanted to see his face in them.

Needless to say, one or the other of us was constantly
serving seven days confined to barracks, and we naturally took turns to do it. If, for example, John was given
seven days, he would do the first four, and George the
other three. The Provost Sergeant soon found that he
was frequently sorting out which one of us was cur-
rently doing the seven days, and ensuring that the
right one turned up. "Don't try and fool me," he
roared at one of us on a certain occasion, "because I
can tell you two apart even if nobody else can; just

watch yer step and don't try swopping over, see!" But
we had already swopped over; he was already talking
to the wrong one. What little hair the Provost Sergeant
had soon turned gray, then fell out.

About two months after our reunion at Aldershot a
notice was posted on the battalion notice board. It was
headed DRAFT FOR INDIA. Then followed a list of names
of those who had been selected for posting to the 1st
Battalion stationed at Trimulgherry, India. We
scanned the list eagerly to find our names. Yes, there
it was: Private J. R. Newmark. But only one of us!
Private G. H. Newmark was not on the list at all.
Obviously a mistake; they surely wouldn't send only
one of us. Or would they? A nasty tinge of suspicion
crept into our thoughts. Had the Provost Sergeant
made an official complaint? Had he suggested one of us
should be posted to India so as to avoid any further
confusion? It seemed highly probable that he was responsible for one of us going and not the other one. He
had frequently told us both to go to all sorts of places.
We took immediate steps to deal with the situation.
First we applied for an interview with the Company
Commander; he was most sympathetic but said there
was nothing he could do. Then we went to the Commanding Officer, who listened attentively to our tale of
woe and offered a brilliant suggestion. He informed us
that, according to military law, if two brothers were in
the Army but in different regiments or battalions, the
elder of the two could claim to have his younger
brother posted to his own regiment or battalion. We
thanked the Commanding Officer, saluted smartly, and
marched out. We immediately went into conference

and drew up our plan of action, but kept it to ourselves. Top secret, we decided. U. S. 1294949

Three weeks later the draft sailed for India, carrying John in high spirits. John was two hours older than George; not very much, but enough. So on the day he set foot on Indian soil, he applied to have brother George transferred to his battalion. The Army had no alternative but to send George out on the next draft; it had to be very careful always to obey its own rules and regulations. So in due course George arrived in India too, and once again we were reunited.

Our ambition was at last realized. We were in the tropics, and the very air around us was filled with strange sounds and even stranger smells. Lizards scuttled about over the ground, gay and colorful butterflies hovered over equally gay and colorful flowers, and birds in brilliant plumage darted in and out among the bushes. We were entranced, and that very first evening, with complete disregard for the orders which had been posted on the notice board—we didn't even know where the board was—we went off together for a walk and listened to the sounds of a tropical night: the incessant whirring of cicadas, the occasional cry of a night bird, and the distant howl of jackals. We listened with joy in our hearts; and as we listened we heard, faintly, the sound of a bugle blowing "lights out."

We hurried back. We simply hadn't noticed the time slipping by. Unfortunately, the Guard Commander noticed us slipping by as we entered the barracks an hour late. Seven days confined to barracks for the pair of us, and another Provost Sergeant discovered to his dismay that he had a pair of twins on his hands, and couldn't tell which was which.

The next few months seemed like one continuous holiday for us. Amidst our military duties, we found numerous opportunities to see something of the wild life which was to be found all around us. The birds, especially, fascinated us and we only had to step outside the barrack room to see kites and vultures sitting on the branches of nearby trees ready to pounce down on anything in the way of food. Hoopoes walked about the stony ground, in a thoroughly casual, offhand manner, looking for insects. But our favorite birds were the beautiful, tiny sunbirds, scarcely any larger than hummingbirds. As they darted about among the flowering shrubs feeding ceaselessly on tiny insects, their plumage shimmered green and bronze every time the sun caught it. They seemed remarkably tame and allowed one to approach to within a couple of feet before darting off to another branch. Then there were the dainty little tree squirrels which chased one another up and down the trees, or even occasionally sat on the barrack room window sills; and the civet cats which lived high up in the rafters of the barrack rooms and only descended after dark. Many a time we had sat up on a moonlit night hoping to catch a glimpse of these rather ghostly creatures.

Of course, we did a certain amount of soldiering, too, when called upon to do so; but, whenever possible, we mingled pleasure with business and seldom went about our military duties without learning something about natural history. Guard duties, for instance, enforced us to stand at ease outside a sentry box, or to pace up and down in the prescribed military style for two hours at a stretch; what better opportunity than this two-hour period in which to record the various

species of birds which inhabited the area visible from
the sentry box? Or again, provided one stood motionless, there were always the lizards to watch, or even
occasionally a snake gliding silently among the orna-
mental palms and shrubs. Extra guard duties were
sometimes given to soldiers as a punishment; we
received our fair share of it, like everyone else. But it
was months before our Company Commander discovered that we thoroughly enjoyed being on guard, and
frequently volunteered for it.

Another of our favorite duties was that of "marker" on the firing range. A marker is the man who stands alongside a soldier firing at a target several hundred yards distant and, with the aid of binoculars, is able to see where the bullet enters the target; then, after each shot, he provides such information as "a little too low," or "your shots are falling short." We always did our best to provide accurate information and, indeed, our observations were generally considered most helpful. But when, as frequently happened, we saw a bird through the binoculars, the man firing the rifle knew nothing of where his shots were going; instead, he learned that "it looks very much like an Egyptian vulture," or that "it probably belongs to the warbler family." To us, binoculars were invented for bird watching; using them to see where bullets went was of secondary importance.

Perhaps it was inevitable that our capacity for keeping pets in unlikely places should lead us into trouble sooner or later. We had for some time cherished the idea of collecting a variety of snakes and lizards and sending them to the London Zoo. However, air transport in those days was not as frequent, nor as efficient, as it is now, and in any case the cost would have been well beyond our means. So we decided that the best we could do would be to start our own Reptile House. Our friend the Quartermaster promised to let us have a few empty biscuit tins and ammunition boxes in due course. In the meantime we found that a spare pair of boots provided very comfortable accommodation temporarily for small snakes and lizards. We each had a spare pair of boots which were kept in a high state of polish, and which were used only for Saturday morning kit inspections. At these inspections every article of clothing had to be laid neatly on the bed, ready for inspection by an officer. The left boot of each pair, we decided, would do nicely for snakes, and the right boot would do for lizards. A rolled-up pair of socks stuffed into the top of each boot would prevent the creatures from escaping, while the holes for bootlaces would provide ventilation.

Lizards were common everywhere, and it was not long before the right boots were occupied by several varieties. We fed the reptiles every day on small insects, and they seemed quite content to live in a boot. Each Saturday morning kit inspection came and went, and the inspecting officer remained quite unaware that the boots contained anything at all. Indeed, we were congratulated on their high state of polish.

Then one Saturday morning a very young lieutenant just out from England held a kit inspection, and to show how frightfully efficient he was he inspected not only the outside of the boots but the inside as well. We just had time to remove all the lizards and stuff them into our pockets, but there was no time to rescue a snake before the officer had reached our beds. We had caught the snake only the previous day, and now it lay peacefully in the toe of a boot that was about to undergo an inspection.

The officer surveyed our beds. Our kits looked exceedingly smart all laid out in correct military fashion, and the boots gleamed like mirrors.

"That's what I like to see," said the young lieutenant, picking up one of the boots. "Some really hard work has gone into that. Jolly good show."

He was about to discover that some really hard work was not the only thing that had gone into the boot. He peered inside and removed the sock.

"Good heavens!" he exclaimed as the snake slithered out and fell to the floor. "A cobra! It's a cobra!" He dropped the boot hurriedly and stood back a few paces, pale and shaken, and fumbled for his revolver.

"Oh, that's nothing, sir," one of us told him in a casual tone. "You often find snakes in boots out here."

"And scorpions, too," added the other one by way of starting a discussion on natural history. We felt it was unnecessary to assure the young officer that the snake was not a cobra, but was a harmless variety known as a Racer. We hoped to discourage him from inspecting boots.

He returned the revolver to its holster, and resumed his inspection with rather less enthusiasm and considerably more caution.

Shortly after the snake-in-the-boot affair, another small incident occurred, due entirely to the high regard we had for the smaller creatures of this earth. This time it concerned a spider. It was only a small one, but prettily colored in a rather attractive shade of beige. John first noticed it crawling up his rifle when he was on sentry duty outside the guardroom. He watched it climb right up to the top, pause for a moment, and then disappear down into the barrel. John thereupon came to the conclusion that his rifle barrel was an eminently suitable place in which to keep the spider. So there it lived for several days. Now and again it emerged from the end of the barrel, took a breath of fresh air, so to speak, then disappeared inside again. It was quite out of the question, of course, to clean the rifle. This was normally done by pulling a small piece of cloth right through from one end of the barrel to the other, but with a spider reposing peacefully inside, it was impossible to perform this operation. The barrel remained neglected gathering dirt each day.

It was inevitable that there would be a rifle inspection before long. It was carried out by a sergeant major who rejoiced at the very thought of finding even one speck of dust in a rifle barrel. John's platoon was lined up, and the sergeant major went down the line, inspecting each rifle in turn, till at length he reached John. All might have been well if the spider had pressed itself flat against the side while the sergeant major peered down the barrel from the muzzle end.

But no; it had to choose that particular moment to walk out for another breath of fresh air.

For an instant the spider and the sergeant major looked at each other. Then, as an expression of sheer incredulity spread across his rapidly reddening face, he exploded. The stream of language that followed was a remarkable lesson in the use of unfamiliar adjectives, and John heard himself described in picturesque terms totally new to him, though plainly understood.

Thus began another period of seven days confined to barracks, of which John did the first four, and George the remaining three.

G.A.G.

5: Secret Weapons

Our activities in the field of natural history came to a temporary stoppage on September 3, 1939, the day that England went to war against Germany. We felt that our military duties now exceeded all others, and it was with a good deal of reluctance that we put away our books on zoology and started reading such works as *A Manual of Military Strategy,* or *The Duties of a Commander in the Field.* We weren't Commanders by a long shot, though we had reached the lofty rank of sergeant. However, since our country was now at war, we decided that it was faintly possible that the War Office might be willing to take the risk of promoting us to something a good deal higher. After all, we had served in India, Palestine and Malta, and we now felt that the time had come to apply for a Commission. Hitler, however, decreed otherwise and proceeded to capture not only France, but George as well, as he happened to be in that country training a territorial battalion. John was still at Malta, preparing to defend the Island against an invasion by the Italians. He did, in due course, gain a Commission and finally reached the rank of Captain. George, however, found himself being bundled off into a prisoner-of-war camp in the heart of Germany where he remained for the next five dismal years. Even there, however, his undiminished love of insects played a slight, though hitherto unrecorded, part in winning the war. He found that the whole camp was infested with lice; there wasn't a man in the camp who could claim to be entirely free of them. So, as it was impossible to remain liceless for any length of time, George decided to collect them. He merely had to examine the seams of his clothing to be sure of finding a dozen or so. Since there were a couple of thousand other prisoners in the camp, all of whom possessed a similar quantity of lice, it wasn't long before he had several tins full of the insects.

Now it so happened that George, together with twenty other prisoners, was sent out every day on a working party, and one of the jobs this particular party had to do was to unload coal from railway wagons

onto lorries, then accompany the lorries several miles away to a German barracks and again unload the coal into cellars. To reach the cellars, four or five of the prisoners, including George, were taken through one of the barrack rooms which contained sleeping quarters for thirty German soldiers, then down some steps which led into the cellar. There, the prisoners were left by the guard to work in the cellar, the guard returning to the lorry to supervise the unloading of the coal. And it was during this period without a guard that George returned to the barrack room containing thirty beds, and emptied his tins of lice into them at discreet intervals. There is no record of the number of lice, which, in this manner, were transferred to enemy lines, nor is there any means of estimating the acute discomfort caused to the occupants of those beds; but if only one of those lice irritated only one German soldier to such an extent that he shouted, "To Hell with Hitler!" instead of "Heil, Hitler!" then it was a blow struck in the defense of freedom.

George became rather fond of his lice; he also became quite skilled in the surreptitious disposal of them. Thousands went into enemy beds as related above; others—perhaps a matchbox full at a time—were gently tipped into the jack boots of German officers. On one occasion, the Camp Commandant himself became a victim of a "louse raid." Every day he held an inspection of the camp. The prisoners were lined up in their huts, counted by the guard in charge, who then reported to the Commandant that all was ready for inspection. At this point, the Commandant always took off his heavy military overcoat and handed it to an orderly who carefully hung it up from a hook

near where the prisoners were lined up. This procedure never varied, and George saw his opportunity.
He filled a matchbox full of lice—fine, muscular ones
specially selected for the occasion—and stood in line
only a foot away from the overcoat; and when the
Commandant was down at the other end of the hut, it
was a simple matter for George to take one step back,
empty the matchbox into the folds of the overcoat,
and return to his position, mission accomplished.

George continued to deposit lice among the Ger-
mans for many months before he was transferred to
another camp, together with the rest of the working
party. There, somewhat to his dismay, he found the
conditions were more hygienic, and only an occasional
louse came his way.

In the meantime John waged war in a more ortho-
dox manner, first in Malta where he fired his rifle in the
general direction of the sky whenever enemy planes
came over to bomb the island; then in France with
the invasion forces where he aimed in a general easterly
direction. But in due course he, too, was captured
together with twenty-six men and a major who was in
command of this small force. They had spent a night
in a wood, isolated from the rest of the battalion, but
in touch by wireless. Early the following morning, as
daylight filtered through the trees, heavy firing was
heard coming from all directions, and the major in
command ordered a general stand-to. John, who was
responsible for the wireless, quickly flashed a message
to Headquarters asking for reinforcements. The wireless set was in a small hut, and when he peered around
the doorway to see what was going on, he found the

major and his twenty-six men lined up in a row, and in the process of being searched by a German officer, while German troops stood on guard in menacing attitudes. John, who had not yet had breakfast, quickly ate a secret document, smashed up the wireless by treading all over it, and just had time to destroy his maps before he was discovered.

On the long six-day trek to a prisoner-of-war camp in Germany, John learned that the small party of twenty-six men and the major, isolated as they were in the woods, had been surrounded by over three hundred German troops who had stumbled across them by accident. Whether the reinforcements he had asked for before treading on the wireless ever arrived was never discovered, for the prisoners were whisked away without delay.

Thus it was that John found himself in a prisoner-of-war camp in Germany. For lack of anything else to do, and because of his interest in insects, he turned his attention to the study of fleas and bedbugs. There was certainly no shortage of them, and before long other prisoners were bringing him a regular supply.

It is extraordinary how twins, especially identical twins, think alike and act alike, even though they may be separated, miles apart from each other and completely out of touch. George was in one prisoner-of-war camp, John was in another. George collected lice, John collected bedbugs. George disposed of his lice by presenting them to the enemy. John did precisely the same with his bedbugs, though he adopted a different method. He gathered his specimens together, graded them according to size, wrapped them neatly in toilet paper, a dozen or so at a time, and sealed them up in envelopes. The envelopes were then addressed to selected German officers in charge of the guards, and placed in the mailbag for delivery. He took a certain delight in making sure that the largest and most bulging of the bedbugs went to the largest and most bulging officers.

Not until the end of the war did John and George meet again, and only then did they discover how similar their actions had been, and how they had both waged their own private war on the enemy and, it is hoped, caused a certain amount of discomfort and irritation.

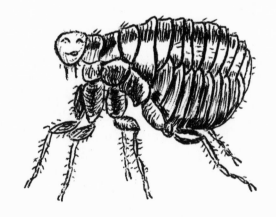

6: 🚶🚶 Meet Mr. Ng

In August 1945, World War II came to an end and a sigh of relief went up all over the world. We had already been flown back to England, together with thousands of other prisoners of war, and given a long period of leave. Shortly after this our military career came to an end and another sigh of relief went up, this time from the War Office and, no doubt, all the Provost Sergeants in the British Army.

Although we were now out of the Army, the urge to travel was still with us and we began to consider what prospects there were abroad for civilians. At about this period, a circular issued by the Colonial Office came to our notice; it stated that certain Government appointments were vacant in Malaya, and that preference would be given to ex-soldiers. We were both ex-soldiers; we both applied to the Colonial Office; and we were both accepted. Three weeks later we landed at Singapore.

India had fascinated us during our Army days; but Malaya was a perfect paradise for the naturalist. Even if you lived in one of its teeming cities such as Kuala Lumpur, or Penang, or Malacca, you were never far from the rich, evergreen forest which covers two-thirds of the entire country. In Kuala Lumpur itself, the world's largest moth, the Atlas, could often be seen fluttering around the lamp posts at night; and if you left your window open and the light on, enormous beetles, almost the size of matchboxes, would hurtle through the air as if jet propelled and crash into the walls or the ceiling, generally without apparent damage to themselves, though occasionally they would knock themselves out and fall to the floor with a thud. Small lizards ran about the ceiling upside down, snapping up flies and other insects that settled there; we soon learned to regard these lizards as extremely useful and friendly little creatures, since they were very much on our side in the ceaseless war against the mosquito menace.

In the jungle were to be found such delights as the world's largest snakes, birds that bark like a dog, lizards that fly, insects that scream, and some of the most colorful birds to be found anywhere on earth.

We both felt that the time had at last come when we could really collect unusual reptiles and insects and send them to the London Zoo. We made inquiries at the Singapore airport as to how to go about sending livestock, and were informed that a plane left once a week, carrying a wide variety of animals: dogs, monkeys, birds, and an occasional leopard or tiger. Certain forms would have to be filled in, of course, and a health certificate produced for every animal traveling. All very simple, we were assured.

Nevertheless, we felt far from being reassured since our intentions were to send snakes and lizards and beetles and scorpions. Who would supply a health certificate for these sorts of creatures? Who could certify that a snake, possibly of a poisonous variety, was in the very best of health and not suffering from tonsillitis? Or that a toad hadn't high blood pressure? Or a bright green beetle yellow jaundice? We envisaged difficulties ahead.

During one of our trips into Singapore, we came across several pet shops where a wide variety of birds were sold to the general public. We made it our business to become acquainted with the manager of the largest shop and establish friendly relations. He, being Chinese, made it his business to extract from us every penny that we were willing, or even unwilling, to part with, in return for which he would endeavor to obtain for us certain birds which we were particularly anxious to send to London. Nothing, however, would induce him to open a snake department, in spite of our offering guaranteed prices for every single snake he caught.

"Me velly afraid of snakes," he explained apologetically, "but I sell you plenty velly good birds velly cheap."

The first "velly good bird" we acquired from our shopkeeper friend, Mr. Ng, was a Black-naped Oriole, a bird which the Zoo had exhibited only once before. After the usual haggling over the price—we had become skilled and experienced hagglers during our

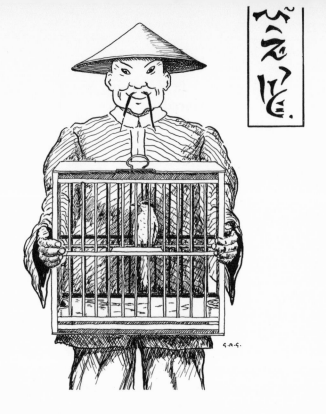

Army days in India—we purchased the Oriole and a small bamboo cage in which to send the bird to London.

Next, we presented the bird to the Government Veterinary Department in order that one of its Officers could certify that it had neither mumps nor chicken-pox. The Officer looked at the bird and informed us that he had never seen one quite like it before; for this reason, if for no other, the Oriole successfully passed its medical inspection, and we moved on to the next stage in the process of sending it to London. This was at the airport, where numerous forms had to be filled in, all in triplicate; instructions had to be pasted on the outside of the cage, giving information as to what food the bird required during its journey; and sufficient quantity of the food had to be supplied, as well as a suitable container for water. Finally, a heated discussion broke out among the Chinese authorities as to whether the cost of sending the bird was determined by the cubic measurement of the cage, or by the weight of bird and cage.

Obviously, if somebody was sending a very small bird in a very large cage, the whole thing would weigh next to nothing, but would nevertheless occupy a considerable space on the plane; on the other hand, if somebody sent a very large bird in a very small cage, it would take up only a small amount of space, but would weigh quite a lot. And, just to simplify matters, we pointed out that if a large bird chose to jump off its perch and hover in mid-air at the precise moment that the cage was being weighed, its own weight would not be registered. Our observation was discreetly ignored as being unhelpful, and the Oriole was removed from the weighing-in room, shrieking its loudest. We never did discover how the price was finally fixed; perhaps they tossed up. Anyway, the bird eventually departed, and in due course we received notification that it had arrived safely in London, still shrieking.

Highly elated at having at last succeeded in presenting the Zoo with something they really wanted, we kept our eyes on Mr. Ng and his pet shop, and it wasn't long before he obtained another Black-naped Oriole. The first one had been a female; this one was a male, dressed in rich, vivid yellow with black wings and a black stripe through the eye—truly a beautiful and brilliantly colored bird. Mr. Ng felt reasonably sure that he could charge twice as much for the male, and proceeded to do so. We politely brought to his notice the fact that although the male was undoubtedly much more colorful than the female, it would, alas, never lay an egg; only the female could perform that operation, and, to such an august society as The Zoological Society of London, females were of more value than males. Mr. Ng knew instinctively that he was going to lose the argument, and shrugged his shoulders.

"I go bankrupt for you," he wailed, counting the dollars we handed over. While he wailed, we hailed a passing taxi and took the bird home. And once again, in due course, we received a letter of thanks from the London Zoo, as well as another letter from Mr. John Yealland, Curator of Birds, who was delighted that we had managed to obtain a pair of Black-naped Orioles for the Bird House.

From then on, a succession of rare or gaily colored birds migrated from the overcrowded conditions of Mr. Ng's pet shop to the more refined and genteel atmosphere of Mr. Yealland's surroundings, where they spent several happy years in the roomy and heated aviaries of the Bird House.

Our thoughts wandered back to the day, thirty years before, when we had vainly tried to present Toosie the tortoise to the Zoo; on that day, Toosie had been rejected by the authorities, though nevertheless presented by us; perhaps dumped would be a more accurate word. No letter of thanks came our way, and no label went up on that occasion. Now, when we were some eight thousand miles away, labels began to appear on a number of cages and aviaries announcing the fact that a Black-naped Oriole or a Blue-crowned Barbet or a Javanese Brahminy Kite had been presented by

J. R. and G. H. Newmark. Our elevation to the rank
of Zoo Collectors had commenced.

In between dispatching birds, we did some work. It
should be emphasized that collecting for the Zoo was
purely a hobby, and still is; but it is a hobby with a
difference, and if anyone ever organizes a competition
for people with unusual hobbies, we shall certainly
enter.

Six days a week we worked as Government officers;
on the seventh day, and whenever we had a free week-
end, we became Zoo collectors. As already mentioned,
most of our birds were obtained from the illustrious
Mr. Ng, whose beam became broader and broader each
time he produced the bird we wanted. There were, of
course, many occasions when he was unable to obtain
certain birds, but he still beamed at the mere sight of
us approaching his shop.

We frequently asked him to go in for snakes as well
as birds, but Mr. Ng was quite adamant; he was velly,
velly afraid of snakes and wanted nothing to do with
them. So whenever we were free we went off into the
rice fields or the outskirts of the town and searched for
snakes ourselves. We also visited a nearby patch of
jungle, but strangely enough we found most of our
snakes in areas quite close to the town rather than in
the jungle itself. Our Chinese cook, Chew Boon Beng,
also found snakes from time to time either in our
garden or sometimes even in the bungalow.

One day the telephone rang. Mr. Ng was on the
other end and his voice was high-pitched and urgent.

"I have a box full of snakes; come quick, I velly
afraid!"

He gave us no indication as to how many snakes he

had in the box, nor what sort they were. In any case all snakes were deadly poisonous as far as Mr. Ng was concerned. So in case any of them were in fact poisonous, we took our leather gloves and caught the next bus to Singapore, where we found a terrified Mr. Ng standing on the pavement outside his pet shop, which was closed. He beamed as usual when he saw us, but it wasn't his usual beam; it was bent in the middle. We asked him why his shop was closed.

"Snakes inside shop, so I stay outside," he replied in a whisper. "I no want to see them."

He opened the door of the shop and pointed to a distant corner. There we saw a wooden box, with small mesh wire netting at each end and across the top. On closer inspection we saw a number of snakes inside, tangled up in coils around each other so that it was very difficult to tell how many there were altogether. They appeared to be of one species which we recognized at once as the very beautiful Black and Gold Tree Snake—poisonous, though not dangerously so. As far as it was possible to judge in the semidarkness of the box, there were perhaps five or six of them, and all seemed to be about the same size; something around four feet, judging from the thickness of the coils.

Mr. Ng's business instincts began to return.

"I sell you snakes velly cheap," he said, standing a safe distance away. "Flee dollars each. Velly cheap," he repeated.

"Three dollars each?" we queried, knowing full well that Mr. Ng would gladly have given us three dollars merely to take them away. Mr. Ng knew it too, but it is the Chinese custom to bargain over a price, and it is considered impolite to buy anything without an argu-

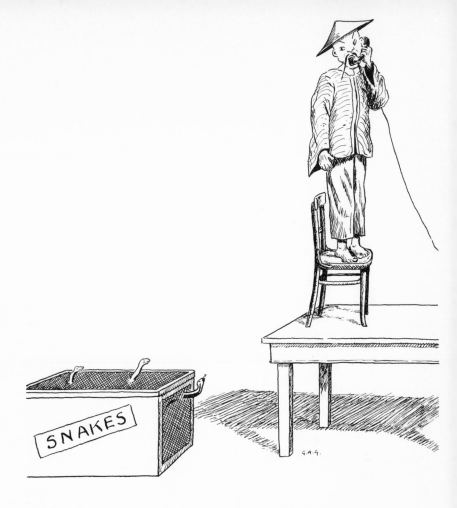

ment. However, we could see that poor Mr. Ng was still terrified at being in the presence of snakes, and we had no wish to prolong either the argument or the agony.

"One dollar each," we announced in a tone which clearly indicated that the bargaining was over. Mr. Ng's beam returned to normal. As far as he was concerned snakes were not only unspeakable; they were unsalable. And yet he had managed to sell them to us.

The box was too large and heavy for us to carry back,

so we decided to transfer the snakes into a pillowcase which we had brought with us for that purpose. Putting on our leather gloves, we started to cut through the wire netting with pliers, while Mr. Ng, fearing the worst, retreated through the door and on to the pavement again where he proceeded to shake.

The snakes offered little resistance. They had evidently been in the box for several days with neither food nor water, and apparently ceased to care what happened to them. We picked them up one by one and placed them carefully in the bottom of the pillowcase. There were five altogether, but one of them appeared to be more dead than alive. We hoped the other four at least would survive.

When the box was empty, we tied the pillowcase securely at the top and walked out of the shop. Mr. Ng still shook on the pavement, and he too appeared more dead than alive. However, he brightened up instantly when he realized we had removed all the snakes, and became very much alive as we handed him the five dollars. He reopened his shop when we were a safe distance away.

We caught the next bus back to our house in Johore. It should perhaps be mentioned that when Chinese passengers board a bus in Singapore, many of them carry all sorts of things done up in all sorts of bundles. Even chickens are sometimes included. As most of the passengers on our bus were Chinese, nobody took the slightest notice when we climbed on board carrying a pillowcase. But then nobody knew what was in it, which was just as well.

Back in our home in Johore we turned our five newly acquired snakes into a large cage and presented

A yard and a half of Royal Python

them each with an egg for lunch. It was some time
before any of them seemed to realize that they were at
last being fed, but once they found the energy to eat
their first egg, their recovery was rapid, except for the
one that was apparently too weak to eat anything at
all. It was dead the next morning. However, we still
had four, and within a short space of time they were
looking beautifully sleek and shiny. In addition to
these four we ourselves had collected six other snakes
of different species, and Chew Boon Beng had found
two in the bungalow. So we now had a dozen snakes
which would make a nice parcel for Mr. Reginald Lan-

worn, Overseer of the Reptile House at the London Zoo.

Mr. Lanworn had previously given us detailed instructions concerning the best method of sending snakes. We carried out these instructions to the letter, and placed each snake in a small cotton bag, tied the bag securely at the top, and then hung each one from small hooks placed around the inside of a specially constructed wooden box. In this manner the snakes would travel quite happily, each suspended in its own bag. All they required on the journey was an occasional dampening which could be done very simply by sprinkling water over the bags. No need whatever to open them up at all.

Before securing the parcel ready for despatch, we had to take it to the veterinary department. The officer on duty there was an Indian gentleman with a beard.

"Good morning," we greeted him jovially as we entered the office. "We have some livestock here which we propose sending to London. Would you mind just having a look and passing it as fit?"

We hoped he wouldn't have a fit. We held up the box for his inspection, and he peered inside, but could only see the cotton bags hanging from hooks.

"Where are the animals?" he inquired, a trifle puzzled.

"Oh, they are inside the bags," we explained, casually. "Each bag contains a snake, you see, and they are all ready to be sent to London, but the air authorities won't accept them unless they have been certified as fit. If you can't certify them, we shall just have to leave them here, and that would be rather a pity."

The Indian gentleman remained calm, though his

beard began to quiver. He sat down at his desk and proceeded to write out a health certificate without any further interest in the contents of the box. He wrote neatly and slowly, and when the document was complete he signed it, stamped it, and handed it to us.

"Gentlemen," he began in quiet, suave tones, "I haven't the slightest doubt that your snakes are fit. I trust both of you are, too."

It was difficult to know whether he was merely being courteous, or whether this last remark was intended to indicate that he included us in his routine inspection of cats and dogs and horses. However, we explained why we were sending the snakes to London, and added that we hoped to send another consignment before long.

"If you want to send any more snakes," he said as we parted company, "just ring me up and I'll send you a health certificate through the post."

We did, in fact, send many more reptiles after that, though Mr. Ng never supplied us with any others. We collected our own snakes and lizards and were particularly gratified on hearing that some of our specimens had never before been exhibited at the London Zoo. This also applied to some of the birds.

In 1957 Malaya gained her Independence, and we returned to England. Two years later we went to Morocco on our first holiday collecting trip.

7: 👥 Bathroom Occupied

Among other problems which may confront the would-be collector is the rather important one of where and how to accommodate your collection; it is a problem which becomes quite delicate if you yourself are accommodated in a hotel, which is likely to be the case when you are on holiday. If it should be a fairly small and not too dressy sort of hotel, the problem is not too difficult; you simply discuss it with the manager and come to an arrangement. But if it is a first-class hotel, the sort that calls itself *de luxe* and has five stars against its name in the guide book, then you really have a problem, and to discuss it with the manager is probably the worst thing to do.

We met the problem during our very first collecting-while-on-holiday trip to Morocco. We were accompanied by Edna, one of our sisters, and Anne, a friend of hers and an aunt by marriage. Edna had often expressed a wish to do a spot of traveling, and she particularly wanted to visit the Middle East. Now Morocco is certainly not the Middle East; it happens to be south, but it is inhabited by Arabs, and that was good enough for Edna who fancied herself riding a camel across the desert. Anne went partly to keep Edna company, and partly because she also had a strong desire to visit a country outside Europe. We had made it very clear at the start that we had no intention of spending our entire holiday in the shopping center of Tangier, which would certainly attract Edna and Anne.

They made it equally clear that they would quite definitely not accompany us on our insect hunts, and wanted absolutely nothing to do with our bugs and beetles. They earnestly hoped that we wouldn't find any.

So it was that we found ourselves in a very nicely situated hotel in Tangier overlooking the bay. It was not the five-star *de luxe* type of hotel, but it was very clean and comfortable nevertheless, and from our rooms we were able to look out across the bay toward Spain. We occupied two double rooms, each with a bathroom attached. *Très élégant.* For the first few days all four of us kept more or less together and behaved very much as tourists normally behave, exploring the town, visiting the *suks,* and spending all our money on souvenirs in the shops. But after a few days we trod separate paths. Edna and Anne continued to gaze in rapture at the shops, while we began doing things which no tourist normally thinks of doing. We began collecting. We were no longer normal tourists; we had become collectors, and when Edna and Anne went off together to do some more shopping in the bazaars which abound in Tangier, we made off in the opposite direction toward the countryside, where our bugs and beetles would abound.

We found plenty. Our main hunting ground was only a mile or so from the hotel, and we gathered an assorted collection of reptiles and insects each day, and brought them back in plastic boxes to our room. But it very soon became evident that we would have to utilize the resources of the bathroom. Being a good-class hotel, we had a good-class bathroom. First, there was the bath itself; absolutely ideal for the turtle which we had found only that very morning in a muddy stream not far away. We could easily place a few rocks in the deep end for the turtle to sit on when it felt the need. The shallow end would do very nicely for the four Moroccan toads which were badly in need of more space. Then there was the hand basin which was nice and deep and wide; pure luxury for our newts and salamanders. They too could be supplied with a couple of flat-topped rocks upon which they could bask or climb about. The gentleman who designed the hand basin must have had us very much in mind, for he gave it a broad flat edge, sufficiently wide to allow a considerable number of plastic boxes to be placed all around it. Other containers could be stacked neatly on the glass shelf over the basin. Finally, there was the bidet, or foot bath, an adornment seldom seen in English bathrooms. Tastefully furnished with a few clods of earth and a sprinkling of grass, it would be eminently suitable for our growing collection of beetles. Behind the door the management had thoughtfully provided three large hooks and a towel rail, obviously intended for our snake bags to hang from in decorative abandon.

We had originally hoped to accommodate all our livestock in the plastic boxes, but as all our sixty boxes were filled within the first ten days, it was plain that we would have no alternative but to commandeer the bathroom. It was a Sunday; a convenient day for rehousing our collection, for the manager of the hotel would be having an afternoon nap, and the rest of the staff would be sufficiently loyal to follow his example. We would not be disturbed.

The turtle was the first to enjoy its new surroundings. It took to the bath instantly and was delighted to be able to stretch its legs and swim the whole length. The four fat Moroccan toads went in, too, and chased each other in circles round the plug. The newts and salamanders had fun trying to climb the slippery slopes of the wash basin, while the beetles made merry in the foot bath, exploring every tuft of grass and digging into the clods of earth. We discovered a couple of large enamel basins in a cupboard, and these provided admirable playgrounds for some of our lizards. The snakes slept soundly in their cotton bags suspended from the hooks and the towel rail behind the door. One snake, the smallest of all, hung daintily from the toilet chain. And the tumbler, which normally contained a toothbrush, was occupied by a tiny frog instead.

Our bathroom must have presented a strange spectacle to Edna and Anne when we escorted them in to show them what we had done. All good collectors put the care and welfare of their animals first, and this invasion of the bathroom meant that we would be unable to use it for ourselves; neither of us intended sharing the bath with four warty-looking toads and a turtle. However, after their first shock, Edna and Anne came to our rescue by offering us the use of their bathroom, which was truly noble of them.

The next problem was to feed our collection. This turned out to be a fairly simple matter because most of their requirements appeared on the dinner menu each evening. There was always a salad which included meat, lettuce, and a variety of vegetables, all very nourishing for most of our creatures. All we had to do was to wrap a slice of meat, a few lettuce leaves, and a tomato into one of the serviettes, pop the lot into Edna's handbag, and leave the dining room at the end of our meal, smiling affably and nodding with the utmost grace to everyone in general. We carried out this procedure each evening, and each evening as we passed the head waiter on our way out he would bow politely and ask whether we had enjoyed our dinner and was there anything further we required? We dearly wanted to tell him that our lizards would have preferred a handful of nice juicy mealworms instead of thin slices of cold meat, and that the beetles adored his lettuce leaves and tomatoes; but we refrained from doing so, and merely answered that the dinner was most enjoyable.

It must be recorded, with deepest sorrow, that the state of our bathroom was nothing compared with the state of the maid when she went in on the Monday morning to clean it out. We had hoped to explain to her before she went in that it was totally unnecessary for her to set foot in the bathroom at all, and that we would look after it until we left the hotel. To our dismay, however, we discovered that she only spoke French and a little Arabic; we of course spoke no Arabic and only a little French. Our French was limited to such words as *pourquoi, au revoir,* and *voulez-vous,* none of which would have been of great assistance in explaining to her that our bathroom was occupied by reptiles and insects, and that she was not to worry about a thing. Those were our intentions. As it turned out, however, we never had a chance to explain anything at all. We were sitting on our beds that Monday morning. There was a knock on the door, but before we were able to reply, she was already in with her mop and her bucket, and making straight for the bathroom. Her whole attitude gave us the impression that it was her bathroom, not ours; a formidable and determined woman, obviously devoted to the bathroom.

We sat on our beds in agony and watched her go in. There was a moment of silence, followed by a shriek that must have been heard in New Zealand. Out she came in a headlong rush, dropping her bucket and mop as she fled, out like a flash through the door, down the stairs and into the street. We believe she went into orbit. She certainly never came near the place again, and neither our bathroom nor the bedroom saw another maid while we remained in the hotel.

It should be added, to our everlasting credit, that when we finally departed at the end of our holiday, homeward bound for the Zoo with our collection, we left our bathroom spotlessly clean and without a trace of turtle or beetle anywhere.

8: A Spider in the Hand

Whenever we go out on a day's collecting, we usually go forth armed with one or two simple items of equipment as a precaution against being bitten or stung by those creatures which delight in biting or stinging their visitors. Of course, professional herpetologists—people who study reptiles—and entomologists —those who study insects—probably know on sight all the dangerous snakes or insects they are likely to come across in whatever part of the globe they are doing their collecting. But we are neither professional herpetologists nor entomologists nor any other sort of ologist; we are schoolmasters acquainted with English, history, and geography, and with a fairly sound general knowledge of snakes and beetles. So we take precautions.

First, we each possess a pair of leather gloves. They may at one time have been fit to wear in the city, but their better days have long since passed. Stained and scratched though they may be, they are nevertheless without any holes, which is an important point. Gloves are very handy when turning over rocks and stones or logs of wood, under which are likely to be found a wide assortment of creatures: snakes, scorpions, centipedes, spiders, and many others. Some of these are likely to be poisonous; whether they are or not, they all resent fingers poking at them or picking them up, and they quite naturally show their resentment by biting the nearest finger. Hence the gloves. It should be understood, however, that gloves are by no means biteproof or stingproof; some snakes could certainly bite through the leather and a scorpion could probably pierce through it with a well-aimed jab. Nevertheless, they do help and one feels far more inclined to pick up a snake by the scruff of its neck if one is wearing gloves.

Next, a good solid pair of walking shoes, and gaiters to protect the lower part of the leg. We have never yet been bitten in the leg, nor have we any desire to be; but if we did perchance step on a snake, doubtless it would become cross and retaliate. For similar reasons, long trousers are preferable to shorts, especially when hunting among thorny bushes and brambles.

Finally, any good mosquito repellent can well be included as an item of equipment. We did on one occasion omit to take any, and the result was disastrous; vast hordes of mosquitos found us, fed upon us, and fattened enormously. It is no exaggeration to state that we were literally driven out of the jungle on that particular occasion.

There was also an occasion when we felt that our leather gloves were more of a hindrance than a help. It happened during that same collecting trip to Morocco, when Edna and Anne were with us. We had all gone to a well-known picnic spot a couple of miles outside Tangier, and known locally as The Mountain. It was a favorite place for the teeming population to visit at weekends, and consisted of an area of high ground overlooking the Straits of Gibraltar. This provided a magnificent view across the Straits into Spain, and, as this was early spring, we were able to watch a number of migratory birds actually making their annual flight from the continent of Africa into Europe. As we sat on the grassy slopes of The Mountain, flocks of brilliant green bee eaters swooped all around us, snapping up insects as they dived, and swallows winged their way over the hill and across the Straits until they disappeared into the haze.

We sat there for an hour or so, enjoying the sun, the scenery, and the sandwiches until there was only the sun and scenery left. Then, leaving Edna and Anne to relax, digest, and turn pink, we decided a gentle stroll among the rocks and boulders might be a profitable pastime. On went our gloves, and out came a few small plastic boxes.

Now it so happened that before leaving England we

Scorpions are quite easy to capture

had asked Mr. George Ashby, Overseer of the Insect House at the Zoo, if there was anything he particularly wanted us to collect while in Morocco, and he had suggested that we might keep an eye open for any large colorful spiders, as well as certain varieties of beetles and scorpions. We had already collected a number of beetles as well as an assortment of scorpions, but we had so far failed to find a single spider sufficiently large or colorful to bother about. We were all the more delighted, therefore, when we came across a nice shapely-looking specimen tucked away comfortably in a crack on the underside of a large rock which we had just turned over. It was not a very large spider, as spiders go, but there was something rather unusual about it. The body was round and smooth and shiny black, as if it had been highly polished; it looked rather like a tiny billiard ball, with legs. We had never come across one quite like it before, and were puzzled as to what kind it was. However, whatever its kind, we decided that it was certainly worthy of our attention and proceeded to plan its capture.

The first problem to solve was how to extract it from its crevice. It appeared to be firmly entrenched and had quite obviously made up its mind to remain there. It looked a rather fragile creature, too, as though it might burst like an overripe berry if it was squashed. To attempt to lift it out bodily was going to be too clumsy an operation to perform with thick gloves on, so off came our gloves. Even then, however, we were still unable to reach the spider which, seeing danger ahead, had retreated to the deepest part of its crack. We tickled its tummy with a small twig and gradually coaxed it out of its crack until it was in such a position that it

A creepy-crawly creepy-crawling

could only crawl into our cupped hands. This it did
with delightful delicacy and there it remained for
several moments while a suitable plastic box was
produced. The box was tastefully furnished with a leaf
or two, and the spider gently deposited into its new
apartment. Peering at it from outside, we noticed with
satisfaction that it had a little patch of scarlet on its
underside, giving it a certain charm and elegance; and

as it was our first capture on The Mountain, as well as the first spider for our collection, we fell in love with it.

After examining our treasure from all angles, we put the box carefully away and continued our search under rocks and stones, first putting our gloves on again as a precaution. We collected quite an assortment of creatures: grasshoppers in various sizes and shades, beetles long and colorful, and a sprinkling of other insects with odd or peculiar shapes. They all went into plastic boxes, and after a couple of hours we returned to the picnic site where we found that Edna and Anne had reached a tender shade of pink and wisely considered that it was time to return to Tangier.

Back in the hotel, we sorted out our catch and transferred several of our creatures, including the billiard ball, into more suitable containers. Edna and Anne were curious to see what we had caught, and were intrigued with the shiny black spider; but when we gently and lovingly turned it out into our hands, Edna shrieked and Anne shrank back, horrified in case it should crawl onto them. In fact, both ladies behaved precisely as ladies generally behave when confronted with a spider. Why this should be is difficult to say, since most spiders are perfectly harmless. Possibly it has something to do with their shape. Whatever it is, Edna and Anne both shuddered in the most feminine manner when we suggested that they might like to hold it for a minute, and were distinctly relieved when we returned it to its plastic home.

In due course, when our holiday was over, the billiard ball was packed away ready for its journey to England, together with a large assemblage of various other specimens we had collected: snakes, lizards, frogs, toads, turtles, grasshoppers, beetles, as well as many other insects which we were unable to identify.

Even though it was early May when we arrived back in England, London Airport was cold compared to the fierce, dry heat of Morocco, and after we had been through the formalities and collected our baggage, we hastened off to the London Zoo as rapidly as possible. There, Mr. Reginald Lanworn, in charge of the Reptile House, took over our snakes and lizards and other reptiles and soon had every one of them identified. Some went on show almost straight away, others went behind the scenes for closer inspection.

Mr. George Ashby, of the Insect House, received his share of the loot with obvious pleasure and proceeded to examine everything with a professional eye. We, being amateurs, were never quite sure when we found a specimen whether it would be on the wanted list or the rejected list; whether it would be received and welcomed with open arms, or merely received with polite thanks, and put aside as suitable food for something else. However, Mr. Ashby seemed very pleased with our collection of insects, and nodded with satisfaction as he removed each one from its plastic box. He is, of course, an entomologist and to him a beetle is not merely a beetle; it is a *Cetonia aurata,* or perhaps an *Aromia moschata;* and as he named each specimen by its correct Latin name, we solemnly nodded in scientific agreement. To us, however, a beetle was a beetle and a spider a spider, whether it was round, square, or oblong, red, white, or transparent.

At length he came to the billiard ball. "Ah," he exclaimed, "just what we wanted! A *Latrodectus!*" A tinge of excitement was detected in his voice. "Where are my tweezers?"

We watched him open a cupboard where four sets of tweezers were hanging on hooks. "Better use these," he continued, selecting the longest of the four. "I don't fancy a *Latrodectus* too close to my bare hands; it is one of the Black Widow family and they are very poisonous indeed, as you probably know."

We did know. Everyone knows that a Black Widow is poisonous, probably the most dangerous spider in the world. But until this moment we did not know that our billard ball was a species of Black Widow. We looked at one another in shocked silence. This was the spider for which we had deliberately taken off our gloves in order to capture it, and then allowed it to crawl about on our hands. This was the spider we had transferred from one box to another, using only our bare hands. This was the spider we had fallen in love with.

"Very poisonous indeed," repeated Mr. Ashby, as he carefully picked up the spider on the end of his longest pair of tweezers, and dropped it safely into its new and permanent home.

We began faintly to understand why females shrink and shudder at the sight of a spider.

9: 👥 Cloak and Dagger Journey on a Bus

It might seem a trifle odd, especially in a book all about collecting small creatures for the Zoo, to devote a whole chapter to the story of a bus trip; but the bus trip itself was sufficiently odd to make it worth while, and it would be a pity to leave it out.

It must be stated, first, that the bus services in Morocco are admirable, particularly the long-distance services. The buses, which keep strictly to a timetable, are reliable; they are clean and reasonably comfortable; the drivers are first class, the roads are excellent and kept in good condition, and the fares are moderate.

Fortified and heartened by this knowledge, we set off early one morning with Edna and Anne and made our way to the coach terminal in Tangier. Our destination was Marrakesh, and the first part of the journey was to be by coach as far as Casablanca. For reasons best known to the authorities, most of the long-distance coaches start early in the morning at a time when even the birds are barely awake. Our bus was due to start its 220-mile journey to Casablanca at 6:30 A.M. We had booked our seats a few days earlier and anticipated no difficulty on that account.

On arrival at the terminal we were gratified to see our coach had not a single passenger in it. This was not surprising as we had arrived a good half-hour before the coach was due to leave. It was desirable to occupy the front seats, and our early arrival would ensure this. Edna and Anne, in the best English tradition, climbed on board first and chose to sit immedi-

ately behind the driver, leaving us the two front seats on the left with a clear and unobstructed view ahead. The conductor, who had appeared from an office in the terminal, beamed broadly when he saw how eager we were to occupy the front seats. He dealt very efficiently with our baggage by hurling it onto the roof. It is the custom on these long trips for passengers' luggage to go on the roof. One does not want to be hampered by a large suitcase on the floor between one's legs, and piling it all on the roof, where it was protected by several tarpaulins, was an excellent alternative.

After a little while more passengers arrived and took their seats. Most of the men wore the usual article of clothing known as a djellebah, which is not unlike an outsize duffle-coat complete with hood, and which Edna even now refers to as a jelly-bar. This more or less covered them completely, except for a small area of face colored something between off-white and smoky black, and generally unshaven. They gave the impression of being mixed up in some cloak-and-dagger, blood-and-thunder story, and it was quite possible that most of them carried a dagger concealed beneath their cloaks. Several of the women wore veils so that not even a small area of face was visible. Others had discarded the veil altogether, but would have looked far better wearing one. Some wore enormous hats, larger than anything ever seen at Ascot, and we were thankful not to be sitting immediately behind one of them.

The first stop was at a point about fifteen miles from Tangier, where there was a Customs post. We were leaving the International Zone and about to enter Morocco proper, and at this point it was necessary for

everyone to go through the Customs in the proper
manner, just the same as though it were a foreign
country. Our driver pulled up behind another coach,
which stood empty. All its passengers were evidently
going through the formalities inside the customs shed.
As far as our coach load was concerned, Edna and Anne
led the way, and we all trooped into the already con-
gested customs shed, adding confusion to chaos. The
room became filled with a milling mass of djellebahs
and hats. Three harassed Customs officials endeavored
to cope. Porters tried to heave their way through the
mass, struggling with suitcases and bundles of baggage.
All the luggage on the roof of our coach had to be
unloaded and brought into the shed to be examined.
Somehow we four managed to keep together, and
together we elbowed and pushed our way to the
counters where the luggage was being checked. We
were asked if we had anything to declare, and we
declared a bunch of bananas. Our suitcases were not
examined for the very good reason that they were
nowhere to be seen, which caused us some anxiety.
However, when we were able to extricate ourselves
from the djellebahs, and found ourselves outside in
the open air, we were relieved to discover our cases
were outside too. The porters had apparently left
them, together with several others, having given up
hope of ever getting them to the counters for inspection.

In due course the formalities, such as they were,
were over, and the mass of passengers sorted themselves
out and returned to their respective coaches. The
luggage was once again stacked on the roof, and
covered with tarpaulins. Anne stood outside the coach

to be sure our cases went onto the right roof, and then joined us in the front seats. All seemed ready to go. All, that is, except the driver who was probably enjoying a cup of coffee somewhere. In any case the other coach would have to leave first; it was ahead of ours and there was no room to maneuver past it. It was rather a shabby-looking coach with the paint-work peeling and a large crack in the rear window. It was certainly not one of the Government coaches; probably a privately owned bus, we concluded. From our seats we could see its passengers, and a grim-looking lot they were too, scowling under their djelle-bahs and looking as though they had just carried out a mass escape from prison. We didn't know it at the time, but before the day was over they were, in fact, going to find themselves in prison. But they didn't know it at the time, either.

As we contemplated the scene, the first coach pulled away and was driven off amid a cloud of dust. No sooner were they out of sight than our driver appeared on the scene, accompanied by three fierce and grim-looking policemen, each armed with a revolver, a rifle, and a band of ammunition slung over a shoulder. It looked very much as though they meant business. They climbed on board our coach, but ignored us completely, much to our relief. To our astonishment, however, instead of occupying the few vacant seats, they stretched themselves out on the floor in the aisle, almost at our feet, and covered themselves with blankets and sacking. Very odd behavior for police-men, we thought, wondering whether by any chance they were about to desert the police force. The other passengers were curious too, but no explanation was

forthcoming from anybody, and we could only specu-
late as to what it was all about.

The driver in the meantime had started the coach
again on its interrupted journey to Casablanca. Up to
this point he had driven at a perfectly respectable
speed. Now, however, he appeared to be under the
impression that he was being chased by Red Indians,
for he hurled his coach along at reckless speed in spite
of the many twists and turns in the road. The next few
miles were nerve-racking in the extreme. Swerving
crazily around each bend, regardless of anything
coming in the opposite direction, we careered down
the road, swaying from one side to the other. We
wondered whether we would sway right off the road
altogether. By sheer good fortune we met nothing
coming the other way, apart from a couple of chickens
which promptly collided with each other in their panic
to get away.

We were becoming most alarmed. Why this sudden
desire to tear along at such a mad pace? And why were
there three heavily armed policemen lying concealed
on the floor of the coach?

Then suddenly, as he maneuvered his coach around
a particularly nasty bend, the driver had to pull up
quickly. We had caught up with the other coach, and
only just avoided running into the back of it. It was
jogging along merrily in the center of the road, and
for the time being our coach had no alternative but to
jog along behind it. There were far too many corners
to attempt to overtake it at this stage, though by
hooting incessantly our driver made it abundantly
clear that he had every intention of shooting ahead at
the first opportunity.

The first opportunity came several minutes later when the road straightened out for some distance. With one foot pressed hard on the accelerator, and a hand pressed hard on the hooter, our driver positively forced his way alongside the other coach until they were racing together, neck and neck. We soon began to draw away, however, in our more powerful vehicle, and before long we were leading, with the other coach close on our tail.

Then suddenly many things happened. Without any warning at all our driver clamped on his brakes, pulling the steering wheel hard over in the same instant. The coach slewed around dangerously and came to a grinding halt at an angle right across the road, blocking it completely. Not even a bicycle could have squeezed by. The coach behind us, brakes jammed on, slithered to a stop within inches of ours. The three policemen who had been lying on the floor under the blankets rapidly came to life, jumped to their feet, pulled their revolvers from their holsters, and flung themselves from the coach, flourishing their pistols and rifles and yelling blue murder. They made a dash toward the coach behind, which by now was discharging passengers from doors and windows like so many ants swarming from an ants' nest. Leaping and tumbling to the ground, they fled in all directions with the policemen in hot pursuit. Away they went, their flowing robes trailing behind them; over bushes and boulders they leaped in a frenzied desire to escape, while the policemen chased after them, lashing out to left and right with rifle butts. Over the top of a hill went some, down into a valley went others, into a forest went some more, until all had disappeared from view save for a few sprawling bodies which lay scattered over the ground where they had tripped over a stump, or been knocked out by a clump on the head with a rifle butt.

All this happened in the space of a few minutes, and we sat there in our seats as though mesmerized. It was almost as though we were watching a film: Bedouin Army in full retreat, Foreign Legion hard on their heels—all in glorious Technicolor. But far from seeing a film, we were witnesses to an extraordinary and thrilling event: the ambush of a band of smugglers.

It was disappointing that we were not able to watch the final roundup, but our driver had a timetable to adhere to. We implored him to stay a little longer at the battleground, but he drove away nevertheless, though this time at a reasonably safe speed.

We learned the rest of the story from the newspapers the next morning. The smugglers had carried on a traffic in drugs and cigarettes for some time, using that same delapidated coach for their unlawful operations all the time. The authorities became suspicious, and organized the ambush in which we had played a part merely as bystanders. The ambush had been planned to take place precisely where it occurred, for a cordon of police and troops encircled the area, though at some distance and out of sight from the road. The smugglers that escaped the rifle butts of the three policemen must have been trapped later by the police cordon, and the whole gang finished up in gaol.

It was an exciting prelude to our reptile and insect hunting holiday.

10: Second Trip to Morocco

Our first collecting-on-holiday trip to Morocco was highly successful. We had brought back over a hundred creatures for the Zoo, while Edna and Anne between them had collected nearly the same number of souvenirs from the shops and bazaars.

On arrival at the Zoo, all our reptiles were identified by Mr. Lanworn and accommodated in new and spacious homes in the Reptile House. Mr. Ashby received our assortment of insects, scorpions and spiders with glee, and supplied each of them with a new home and a Latin name.

Even before our sun tan had worn off, we were discussing the possibility of another trip to Morocco, this time with Mr. John Yealland, Curator of Birds at the London Zoo, and a bird-watching friend of his, Mr. Ian Schalburg, a schoolmaster at Hill Brow School in

Somerset. We pored over maps, went into details and plotted our route. Our plans, briefly, were to spend the first three days in Tangier, during which time we would take John and Ian to The Mountain where they would be able to watch the migratory birds as we had done the year before with Edna and Anne. We would then travel south to Marrakesh and stay there for four days; this would allow our sun blisters, acquired in Tangier, to burst in comfort. Then farther south still, across the Atlas Mountains and down into the town of Taroudant which lay remote and isolated somewhere in the plains bordering the Sahara. There we hoped to do most of our collecting.

The whole journey there and back would cover a distance of roughly 3,000 miles, traveling by plane, train, coach, ferry, donkey and bicycle.

Everything went according to plan and on Good Friday we started our 3,000-mile journey by catching a No. 74 bus from Baker Street to the air terminal in Kensington. A few hours later we were in Gibraltar, where we boarded the ferry for Tangier.

Our three days in Tangier were devoted almost entirely to bird watching. John Yealland, as ornithologist-in-chief, was able to identify many of the birds which had puzzled us on our previous trip. Warblers are notoriously difficult birds to know, but John's knowledge of them was quite astonishing; indeed, he warbled himself every time he saw one and identified it. Ian, whose specialty was birds of prey, was enthralled with the birds we saw during one early morning walk. Hen Harriers, Marsh Harriers, Black Kite, and Lesser Kestrels are all birds which are rarities in England; we saw the lot before breakfast. On one occasion, Ian merely looked out of our hotel window and saw over a hundred Black Kite circling high in the sky; he was so excited we thought he was going to float out of the window and join them.

On our last day in Tangier, we visited The Mountain. While watching the bee eaters swooping and diving all around us, Ian suddenly exclaimed, "Look! An eagle!" We looked in the direction indicated and saw a large, blackish bird gliding in wide circles over a wooded area not far away. We walked over toward the woods and found it was surrounded by barbed wire. It wasn't difficult to find a gap and in we went. After walking through the woods for a few minutes, we came to a small clearing and saw the eagle directly overhead.

"It looks to me like a Booted Eagle," John remarked

after studying the bird through his binoculars.

"Yes," agreed Ian, "I think you are right." The eagle made a wide sweep which took it over the treetops and out of sight. We followed. Suddenly, we found ourselves surrounded by about a dozen Arabs wearing some sort of uniform and carrying an assortment of firearms. We remained cool, calm, and British as the leader approached us. "What are you doing here?" he asked in French.

John was the only one of our party whose knowledge of French was beyond the *voulez-vous* stage. "Good afternoon," he began in quiet, polite tones. "We are looking for the Booted Eagle; we saw it a little while ago, then lost it. Have you ever seen a Booted Eagle?"

It was quite plain that the Arab was far more interested in us than he was in Booted Eagles or any other sort of eagles.

"What are you doing here?" he repeated in rather more menacing tones. The remaining Arabs moved closer in. Just then, Ian spotted the eagle soaring directly overhead again. All four of us ignored the Arab soldiers and focused our binoculars on the bird. The Arabs followed our gaze upward.

"Yes," pronounced John after a pause, "that's a Booted all right; but let's check up with the book." He extracted his *Field Guide to the Birds of Europe* from his haversack and turned to the page illustrating eagles. We compared the bird with the illustrations and satisfied ourselves of its identity beyond doubt. But we still had to satisfy the Arabs of our own identity. John showed them the *Field Guide* which was full of colored illustrations. The soldiers crowded around and turned the pages, making exclamations whenever they saw a picture of a familiar bird. They also took turns looking at the eagle through our binoculars and gasped with astonishment when they saw how close it appeared to be. An international situation was averted by the Booted Eagle.

"But you must go away from here," warned the leader of the Arab party, "as these woods are in the grounds of the French High Commissioner."

We returned to our hotel considerably elated as well as enlightened. That night, we snored in harmony on the train bound for Marrakesh.

Marrakesh provided more thrills of a different nature. We became hopelessly lost in the vast maze of narrow streets that wind for miles through the native quarter of the city, and were rescued by a guide only after paying him a fabulous sum for his services. We visited the famous Mamounia Hotel and sipped cold drinks on the terrace, which cost us another fabulous sum. We dined on the roof of a restaurant overlooking the Djemaa el Fna, an enormous square in the center of the city. The square was filled with several thousand people: Arabs in white djellebahs, Berbers in blue coats, Negroes in gaily colored robes, soldiers in uniform, and children in nothing. As we sampled some unidentified Moroccan dish, an Indian snake charmer sat himself down close to our table and proceeded to charm his snakes. He failed utterly in his efforts to charm us, but when we interrupted him halfway through by offering to buy his largest snake, it was his turn to be charmed. However, negotiations broke down over the price and we returned to our hotel, snakeless.

The snow-capped peaks of the Atlas Mountains,

stretching across the horizon south of Marrakesh, beck-
oned us; and four days later we set off on the seven-
hour journey over the range. Our coach was modern
and comfortable, and was equipped with a radio and
loud-speaker which played Arab-style music loudly and
nonstop throughout the journey. The music may have
been preludes and nocturnes for all we knew; utterly
soothing to Arab ears no doubt, but shattering to ours.
But it served a purpose. The road across the mountains was narrow and winding, zigzagging in a series
of hairpin bends. The Negro driver took the greatest
pleasure in negotiating each bend with casual abandon,
and the purpose of the music was to distract the attention of the highly excitable Arab passengers from the
sheer precipice that dropped a thousand feet or more
alongside certain stretches of the road. Most of the
passengers, however, had their own way of hiding the
drop from view; they simply pulled the hoods of the
djellebahs well down over their heads. We were thankful the driver didn't have a hood.

Occasionally the coach stopped at rest houses built
by the roadside. These stops allowed both the driver
and the engine to cool down, and the passengers to
stretch their legs and perform other necessary deeds.
At one of these stops we four went for a stroll, and
within a few moments a beautifully colored bird flew
into a nearby tree. John raised his binoculars. "Moussier's Redstart," he pronounced without hesitation.

We other three looked at the bird and agreed that
it was unmistakably a Moussier's Redstart; the fact that
we had never even heard of such a bird was purely by
the way. John Yealland certainly knew his birds.

We resumed our journey. The coach continued to

climb for another two hours until at length we reached the highest point, over 6,000 feet above sea level. After a brief halt here, we began the journey down the southern slopes. The radio still blared forth at full strength, but additional volume was now provided by the driver who sang unfamiliar airs at the top of his voice. This was apparently to celebrate the fact that he had successfully accomplished the most hazardous part of the journey, and all his passengers were still with him. As we descended to the lower slopes, we could feel the heat of the plains rising to meet us. The vegetation changed; cactus and thorny scrub dotted the landscape and patches of sand reminded us that the desert was not far distant.

Down on the plains we traveled for another hour, leaving the mountains behind us. Then, quite suddenly, the walled city of Taroudant appeared through the heat haze, and the coach drew up at the gateway to a fort. The driver informed us that our hotel was inside the wall. We disembarked, collected our baggage from the roof of the coach, and entered the gateway. We saw the hotel a short distance inside, and a lady in black stood by the front entrance.

"You are late," she greeted us, in French. She was middle-aged, angular, rather tall, and dressed entirely in black. John politely explained that our coach was exactly on time, and that we would like to be shown to our rooms so that we could have a bath and change. We learned later that the lady had expected us to arrive much earlier in the day by car, and rolling in wealth. When she saw us disembark from an Arab coach, her dream of sudden riches vanished. We christened her the Black Widow.

Our ten days in Taroudant were fully occupied. We did a lot of bird watching, took trips into the countryside on hired bicycles, which never failed to get punctures on every single occasion, and collected quantities of reptiles and insects. We also collected a disreputable gang of tattered Arab youths who frequently appeared at our hotel entrance with all sorts of creatures, mostly half-dead or completely so. The Black Widow looked upon us as a thoroughly dangerous lot as well as utterly crazy, and never came near us. Possibly we smelled. In any case, we were seldom in the hotel so we rarely saw her, which suited both parties admirably.

On one particular day, we decided to go several miles across the sun-baked plains and explore a wooded area which could be seen on the distant horizon; in that sort of country, a wood of any size indicated the presence of water. We hired bicycles for the day and set off shortly after breakfast before the sun was too hot. A narrow track led across the plain toward the woods, and we cycled along quite merrily for about three miles. Then came the first puncture. Before we had completed another mile, we all had punctures, so we left the bicycles in a heap on the track and walked the remaining distance. As we approached the woods, the ground changed from hard, sun-baked sand and rock to coarse green grass and swamp—a pleasant and welcome change. A flock of egrets flew up from the swampy area and John and Ian immediately placed themselves in strategic positions to bird watch. We walked a short distance around the swamp to look for specimens and soon found that the area was rich in beetles. We also collected five large Algerian Skinks,

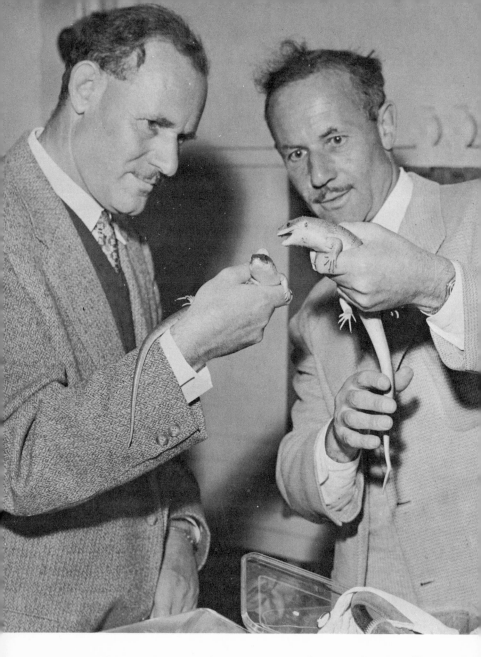

A pair of Algerian Skinks are unpacked in the Reptile House

which are rather attractive gray lizards, mottled with orange. When all our plastic boxes were occupied, we rejoined John and Ian and bird watched with them for several hours.

In the middle of the afternoon, four Arab youths, each on a donkey, approached us. We wished them an extremely good afternoon, whereupon they stopped and one of them produced a rather bedraggled bird from somewhere in the depths of his cloak. John Yealland examined it and identified it as a young Moorish Magpie. It would certainly make a welcome addition to our collection, even though we were not prepared to bring back any birds at all, and after a certain amount of haggling over the price, the magpie changed hands. So did the donkeys, at least for the time being; we felt that the price we were paying for the bird entitled us to the donkeys too, but as we had no desire to present four donkeys to the Zoo, we agreed to borrow them merely long enough to carry us back to Taroudant.

We rode back into town in majestic procession laden with skinks and scorpions, toads and turtles, an imposing assemblage of beetles and spiders, and one squawking Moorish Magpie. We rode through the town, through the gateway into the fort, and right up to the front door of our hotel where a horrified Black Widow stood in the doorway blocking our entrance. She did not remain long; when she saw us unload our specimens, she squawked. We thought it was the magpie that squawked, but shortly afterwards the magpie did squawk and there was a slight difference in tone and pitch.

Our last day in Taroudant was spent in packing our

specimens ready for the long journey back to London. We had collected a total of about 150 reptiles and insects, all of which we finally managed to fit into plastic boxes except the magpie, for which we had to buy a small bamboo cage. Up until the moment of departure, the bird had been given the complete freedom of the bathroom, and it squawked loudly at the indignity of being confined to a cage.

We paid our hotel bill to the Black Widow who actually smiled at us. Whether she did so because we were paying our bill or because we were departing, we never found out.

We returned to Marrakesh the way we had come, over the Atlas Mountains. Our coach again had a radio which blared forth at full pitch as before, only this time the magpie joined in at intervals. From Marrakesh we took the train to Tangier, then the ferry across to Gibraltar, and finally, the night flight to London. At this point we decided that the magpie would have to suffer a further indignity; it was unlikely that the authorities would allow a bird in a cage to travel on a crowded passenger plane. We therefore transferred the magpie from the cage to a small traveling bag with a zipper—the sort which many airlines supply as overnight bags. Thus, the bird became a piece of overnight baggage. Fortunately, no squawks emanated from the bag during the flight. As it was completely dark inside, the magpie no doubt considered it was night. There it remained quite happily until about noon the following day. The bag was then opened and, with an astonished and prolonged shriek, the magpie stepped out and found itself at the London Zoo.

11:  A Night in a Swamp

One of the best times to collect reptiles or insects is at night; there are a great many creatures that are considerably more active after dark than during the hours of daylight. Unfortunately, this includes mosquitoes, and it is even more necessary to take suitable precautions against these pests by night than it is by day. Of all the creatures that inhabit this planet, mosquitoes undoubtedly come well within the top ten for sheer nastiness. So do fleas. If, therefore, you propose to do some collecting at night, give yourself a good thick coating of some insect repellent, not only on your bare bits but over your clothing, too; mosquitoes will find you just as juicy through your shirt as on your bare hands. Wear long sleeves, and long trousers tucked into long socks.

An essential piece of equipment for night hunting is

a good flashlight with a strong beam. An excellent type of flashlight is the sort which fits on a head band, rather like a miner's lamp which he wears when he goes down the pit. This gives you the advantage of having both hands free, though there is also the disadvantage of having to carry a rather bulky battery in your pocket. However, this type of flashlight is particularly handy if you propose to go hunting snakes that live in water. Or frogs. Rubber boots, too, are useful though not essential; they merely add a degree of comfort. You should remember, however, that during the excitement of chasing a snake in water, it is very easy to wade out a little deeper than you intend, with the inevitable result that the water will come pouring in over the top of your rubber boots, and the degree of comfort they hitherto afforded will rapidly vanish.

So, in all probability, will the snake. It is always wise to do a little daylight reconnaissance of the lake or swamp in which you propose to hunt at night, and satisfy yourself that it is not too deep in which to wade.

The first time we ventured forth into a swamp at night was in Florida, when we desired to add a few water snakes to our collection of land varieties. We had been staying with one of our long-suffering sisters, Phyllis, who had a charming and delightful abode in Palm Beach. Perhaps at this point we should make it quite clear for the benefit of the other residents that Palm Beach is quite definitely not the sort of place where one would go to look for snakes; it is far too select and proper for any normal snake to enjoy itself. Every lawn around every house is kept cut at exactly the right level, trees and shrubs are tended with loving care by their devoted and elderly owners, and if even the most adventurous snake dared to show its face from behind some fragrant bush, the police would be instantly informed and the offending reptile removed by an officer of suitable rank. Palm Beach emphatically is not the place for snakes. Nevertheless, we went there since we had no choice in the matter. Phyllis lived there and that was that.

Just across the road from Phyllis lived a gentleman named Fred. Phyllis and Fred were good friends as well as neighbors, and in due course we were introduced. This turned out to be a most fortunate introduction, since Fred, on being told that we were from England and hoped to collect reptiles for the London Zoo, said that he knew of a place not far away where we could find dozens of snakes. Phyllis began to turn a little pale, but regained her tan and her composure when

Fred explained that "not far away" meant a swamp about thirty miles distant.

Plans were made. We would, of course, need a car; Phyllis's would do nicely. On the other hand, Phyllis might not readily take to the idea of using her car to transport a quantity of snakes around the countryside. What would happen if one escaped and disappeared into the depths of the upholstery? She would have fifty fits every time she drove off somewhere. Then Fred suggested that if we were free that evening, he could bring his own car and come with us. So that problem was solved and settled. Fred also knew where he could lay hands on three or four sets of powerful head lamps; excellent—just what we wanted. Finally, a sack and our leather gloves completed the equipment.

Phyllis was not included in our plans; not that we had any difficulty in excluding her, since nothing on earth would have induced her to set her dainty foot in any swamp, snakes or no snakes. She just wasn't the swamp-loving type. She would be perfectly happy to stay at home and watch Perry Mason.

Fred turned up that evening just about dusk, and we set off for the swamp. We reached it about an hour later, by which time it was completely dark. As far as we could see, it was a very wild and desolate stretch of country and the road which had brought us to the area was a very minor one, not much more than a track linking a remote village to the highway several miles east. Just the place for snakes, we thought.

The night was dark and warm, and hundreds of fireflies flickered fairylike over the bushes that grew in and around the water. We gave ourselves a thorough spraying with mosquito repellent, then equipped ourselves

with a head lamp each and a pair of gloves. Finally
when all was ready, we switched on; three powerful
beams stabbed the darkness and lit up three circular
patches of water. We waded in about a foot deep and,
almost at once, made our first capture. "Here's one!"
shouted Fred, bending down swiftly and grabbing a
snake. He pulled it quickly out of the water and
deposited it into the sack. It was soon quite plain that
the swamp was alive with snakes which we could easily
see in the beams of our head lamps; all we had to do
was to bend down and grab one whenever it came near
enough.

For the next half-hour, we bent and grabbed at frequent intervals, and the sack began to weigh quite
heavily. All the snakes we had so far caught appeared
to be of three varieties, all quite harmless. We were a
little nervous at the thought of grabbing a Water
Mocassin, or Cottonmouth as it is sometimes known,
which is a very poisonous snake, and which we knew
lived in the swamps of Florida. But Fred didn't seem
to give any thought to the matter; he just grabbed
anything.

Finally, we decided that we had caught enough; too
many, in fact, since we didn't really want more than
a couple of each variety, and there were already over
two dozen snakes in the sack. However, Fred said that
if there were any we didn't want, he would release
them the next morning in a lake situated between the
fifth and sixth tee on the fashionable golf course in
Palm Beach. "They sometimes create a little diversion,
don't you know," he explained airily. We agreed;
snakes on a golf course can usually be relied upon to
cause a commotion and liven up the game.

On the way back to the car, we found one more snake. It was quite a small one, curled up on a dry sandy patch of ground, and obviously a different species from those we had caught in the swamp.

"Careful!" warned Fred, as our lamps shone down upon the curled, but alert form of the snake. "That's a rattler!" We realized at once that it was indeed a Pygmy Rattlesnake, a variety which we particularly wanted. Before we left London, Mr. Lanworn of the Reptile House had specifically asked us to try and obtain a Pygmy Rattlesnake as the Zoo had not had a specimen for many years. We didn't give this one a chance to think about escaping; bending down swiftly, one of us grabbed the reptile behind its neck, which is the only safe place to hold a poisonous snake, and put it into a plastic box out of harm's way. Spurred on by this piece of good fortune, we looked around for any more that might be lurking nearby. We came to a small wooden bridge spanning a finger of the swamp; a wild profusion of reeds and other water plants grew in the swamp beneath the bridge, and a number of frogs jumped into the water with plops. We captured three of these and popped them into more plastic boxes, and then saw another Pygmy, somewhat larger than the first one. This, too, found itself held firmly behind the neck before being rapidly deposited inside a plastic box.

We considered we had done a good night's work: two Pygmy Rattlesnakes, three frogs of unknown make, and several yards of water snakes which were still in the sack. Just before leaving the swamp to return to the car, we flashed our lamps under the wooden bridge and among the rafters and found, to our delight, a whole mass of cobwebs spun untidily in the corners of the rafters. Every corner had its web, and in the middle of each web sat a big brown blob of a spider. Out came all our remaining plastic boxes, and into each of them went a spider—fourteen altogether.

We drove back to Palm Beach in high spirits, stopping on the way at an all-night coffee shop where we nourished ourselves with steaming hot coffee and footlong hot dogs, about equivalent to a three-course meal.

Phyllis met us on the doorstep of her home and greeted us with the announcement that she too had done a little collecting. She held up a jam jar and revealed yet another spider to add to our collection. We congratulated her and promised that she would undoubtedly be mentioned in despatches back in London. Her smile slid round a corner, however, when she saw Fred standing nearby and holding the sack which writhed suspiciously.

"What's in there?" she asked in tremulous tones.

"Oh, just a few snakes," replied Fred in a disarming manner. "All quite harmless, you know."

Phyllis thought otherwise. "I am not sleeping in the house with a lot of snakes crawling about," she announced firmly. Her tone of voice indicated that she was prepared to take the next plane out of town, regardless of its destination.

There was a moment's pause. Then Fred came to the rescue. "All right, then," he said, "I'll take them over to my place and keep them overnight in the garage."

Phyllis agreed rather reluctantly. Fred lived only a

few doors away; she would have been much happier if he had lived in Alaska.

Fred went back to the car, dumped the sack on the spare seat, and drove off to his home. We retired to our room, Phyllis went to hers. It was nearly two o'clock in the morning and we were well content. So was Fred, in anticipation of letting about a dozen snakes loose on the golf course the next morning. And so was Phyllis, who was quite unaware that the two Pygmy Rattlesnakes, the only dangerous ones of the lot, were in plastic boxes which we had placed discreetly behind a curtain in the bathroom.

12: ♊ Incident on a Plane

Collecting for the Zoo creates a number of problems, quite apart from the task of collecting itself. One of the main points which must be considered is the best method of conveying your animals back to the Zoo and how to pack them ready for the journey. Several other points have to be taken into consideration as well: the length of the journey, which might well vary between two or three hours and a couple of days; whether any food or water is likely to be required during the journey; the possibility of your bags containing livestock being handled carelessly by somebody else; precautions and safeguards against any of your animals escaping *en route*; and possible changes of temperature which are likely to occur between, say, countries bordering the Mediterranean and the chilly expanse of London Airport in midwinter.

Most small creatures can be sent through the post these days, preferably by air mail. This method is quite handy if you should be on a prolonged holiday abroad and you perhaps find some small animal or reptile during the first two or three days, but which you do not wish to keep during the remainder of your holiday. The obvious thing to do then is to send your animal by post. On the other hand, the easiest way to avoid that sort of situation arising is not to start collecting until the last week or so of your holiday.

By far the best way to ensure that your animals get safely to their destination is to carry them with you the whole time. This is positively the only way in which you can be certain that every single creature down to the last bug receives your personal care and attention throughout the journey. Of course, this is only possible if your collection is confined to reptiles, amphibians or insects; such animals as buffaloes or hippopotamuses are inclined to be rather lumpy creatures to carry around and would almost certainly create problems from the excess baggage point of view; so let's leave big game to the professionals and deal only with the smaller creatures. Snakes, for instance. Most snakes under three or four feet in length will travel quite happily in cotton bags securely tied at the top; they are, quite literally, kept in the dark in this manner and generally decide that the most sensible thing to do under such circumstances is to curl up in the bottom of the bag and go to sleep. If, however, you do not possess any cotton bags, plastic boxes will generally do equally well; and although your snake may not feel quite so comfortable in a plastic box, there is the distinct advantage in the fact that it can be seen with-

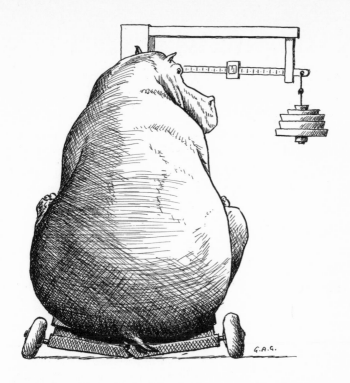

out being disturbed. Plastic boxes and other types of containers will be discussed more fully in a later chapter, but by and large, they can be considered ideal for almost anything you are likely to collect. If you bring back only one or two insects, the boxes can be packed away quite easily among your shirts and forgotten; or, for that matter, they could travel first class in your pocket and perhaps be brought out from time to time to be admired by your fellow passengers. Generally, however, it is probably unwise to let anyone else know that you are carrying a live beetle around, or maybe a spider; many people have a horror of anything that creeps. Worse still, if the lady sitting next to you discovers that the bag between your feet is full of snakes and frogs and things, she might collapse in a heap on top of the bag and damage some of your specimens. Say absolutely nothing; just sit there, wearing a perfectly normal, everyday expression which denotes that your bag contains nothing more interesting than a pair of pajamas, a sponge bag and a book of idylls.

If, on the other hand, you propose to bring back quite a large collection of creatures, which might entail the use of a dozen or more plastic boxes, then it becomes impracticable to pack them all away with your ordinary luggage which, in any case, is liable to be grabbed by a porter and hurled onto a trolley. The only safe method of transporting your livestock from one place to another is, as already mentioned, to carry it with you all the time. We have sometimes carried as many as sixty or seventy plastic boxes around with us, and we have found that ordinary canvas traveling bags are very suitable for the purpose; it is surprising how many boxes they will hold if they are well packed.

Remember one point: that canvas bags are better than the plastic type which tend to get a bit hot inside, and in which some of your specimens might begin to cook. So buy yourself a suitably sized canvas traveling bag—the sort with a zipper on top. Not too large, because you will be carrying it yourself all the time; remember, too, that there is generally not a great deal of room in a coach or a plane. You could use a suitcase if you prefer to, but bear in mind that when you carry a suitcase, you normally hold it by the handle, and the suitcase is then suspended in an upright position; when, however, you board the coach and place the suitcase on the rack above your head, it is then lying flat. This means that the contents of the suitcase are going to be tipped about a certain amount; this could easily lead to bruises or headaches among the beetles.

Of course, mishaps may occur from time to time which are not always possible to foresee. There was the snake, for instance, which felt like taking a little exercise. It happened on our second trip home from Florida, where we had just spent three weeks collecting a large assortment of snakes, lizards, frogs, toads and insects. Most of these creatures had been packed away in plastic boxes except the snakes, which were in cotton bags. Four medium-sized traveling bags held all the boxes—about sixty—quite comfortably, and the cotton bags containing the snakes were placed gently on top of the boxes so as not to be squashed; the zippers were then closed, and there we were ready to board the plane with four perfectly ordinary-looking traveling bags.

In due course our flight number was called and we boarded the plane, found our seats, and sat down with the four traveling bags placed carefully on the floor between our feet. There were three seats in a row on each side of the plane; we occupied the window seat and the middle one, and another gentleman sat on the third seat nearest the aisle. The plane took off shortly after, and we settled down comfortably in our seats for the last lap to London, which would last several hours. After traveling for about one hour, we felt that our livestock could probably do with a bit of fresh air, so we opened the zippers on the traveling bags in order to allow a slight circulation of air to penetrate down among the snake bags and plastic boxes.

The hours dragged on; the engines hummed us into a doze. We slept; the gentleman next to us slept; and the snakes slept—all except one, the one that lay on the very top. This snake apparently couldn't get to

On the way to the airport with bags of livestock

sleep; perhaps flying at a high altitude made it feel a little off-color, or perhaps it merely felt the need to explore its surroundings. In any case, it was securely tied up in its white cotton bag and unable to look around to see what was going on. So, in its efforts to find a way out, the snake wriggled about so much that the bag slipped over the zipper fastener and onto the floor. Had the gentleman in the next seat been awake, he would have beheld the extraordinary sight of a small, shapeless white cotton bag moving about in short jerks on the floor. Fortunately, he continued to sleep soundly, blissfully unaware of what was going on a few inches from his right big toe. Even more fortunately, the bag jerked itself against our own toes and stirred us into consciousness. Dimly aware that a white cotton bag was moving about in spasms beneath our seats, one of us reached down to grab it, but only succeeded in pushing it farther away. Two more jerks, and it was beyond our reach altogether.

We had chosen to occupy the rear seats of the plane. Behind us was a partition which shielded us from all that goes on in the tail of a plane. This same partition now served to halt the bag for a moment, allowing it to contemplate its next move. This it must have done with wicked malice, for it suddenly propelled itself right across the center aisle and disappeared under the seats on the opposite side.

We took immediate action. Climbing over the dozing body of the gentleman next to us, we got down on hands and knees and groveled about between numerous pairs of legs, fearful of the consequences should any of their owners have awakened. Our luck held. Neither the snake nor our groping hands disturbed any legs, and as the bag paused momentarily by somebody's high heel, we grabbed it by a corner. Not without some difficulty did we extricate ourselves from that nylon jungle, triumphantly clutching the offending bag which continued to wriggle as we stood up in the aisle. The other passengers slept on; but our extraordinary activities had attracted the attention of the stewardess, and as we were about to return to our own seats, she spotted the wriggling bag. Her lower jaw dropped a good six inches. We smiled sweetly and muttered something about jumping beans. We also restored her to her senses by ordering two cups of coffee. We needed restoring, too. The gentleman in our row still dozed away quite happily as we climbed back over him. Back in our own seats at last, we returned the snake to its proper place inside the traveling bag, this time closing the zipper fastener firmly over it. No more snake hunting on that plane.

It should be stated here that that particular snake was completely harmless. In case anybody reading this should ever find himself traveling on the same plane with us on a future occasion, we would like to take this opportunity of assuring him that any poisonous snakes we might have in our possession are well taken care of, and would have the utmost difficulty in escaping. Not only are they tied up securely in their white cotton bags, but the bags themselves are then placed in plastic boxes and the lids sealed down. Indeed, on arrival at the Zoo at the end of our collecting trips, the authorities there have more than once commented favorably on the precautions we have taken to ensure that all our livestock arrives safely.

13: 🚶🚶 Vegetable Strainer to the Rescue

One of the joys of going on a collecting expedition is the uncertainty of knowing what you are going to find. There is always the possibility of something rare or curious or even unknown turning up, and it is quite a good plan to expect the unexpected. Not that the unexpected will turn up every time you sally forth on a collecting trip; we have been on several collecting trips, and on two or three occasions have brought back something which caused a mild flutter of excitement in zoological circles. There was the time when we were searching carefully in a pile of wood in somebody's garden in Palm Beach, Florida. The gentleman whose garden we were in had very kindly given us permission to search his woodpile. We were hoping to find a Black Widow spider, and had searched a good many woodpiles in a good many gardens, but without success. The gentleman in question had told us that he had lived there for over forty years, and had never in all that time even heard of a Black Widow spider being found in Palm Beach. Indeed, he made it quite clear that Palm Beach was far too exclusive to allow such creatures to exist in the neighborhood. The residents would protest, probably direct to the President of the United States.

So we set about searching his woodpile, and, sure enough, we found a Black Widow spider. The gentleman was present, too, at that historic moment, but was so astonished that he was not only unable to speak but was unable to move. He stood there, rooted to the spot, dumb with horror; he was almost ashamed that such a creature should be found on *his* woodpile. What would the neighbors say?

We were especially pleased at having found a specimen at all, particularly after being told that Palm Beach was almost out of bounds for such deadly creatures. Maybe half the residents would pack their belongings and move, now that a specimen had come to light. One thing was certain; this gentleman would very soon have his woodpile burned to a cinder. Indeed, those were his first words once he had regained his powers of speech.

Anxious to investigate the wood before it became a heap of ashes, we continued our search. Not until we had reached the very last log right at the bottom of the pile did we find something else: a large creature resembling a stick insect, but about six inches long and as thick as a pencil. There were, in fact, three of these creatures, and we placed them with loving care inside a plastic box, somewhat intrigued as to their identification, and thoroughly satisfied with the morning's work. We thanked the gentleman, who by now had regained a little of his former composure, and returned to our own quarters.

Two weeks later, back at the Zoo, Mr. Ashby was puzzling over the identification of the three creatures, and for once he was baffled. The Zoo had never had them before, and it meant a visit to the Natural History Museum, plus a fair amount of research, before the mystery was cleared up. They turned out to be Florida Walking Sticks, related to the stick insects. The fact that they were new and curious to the Zoo, and had created something of a flurry, was in itself very satisfactory. Even more satisfactory was the fact that before many weeks had passed, they had produced a family of over fifty baby Walking Sticks which were successfully reared on a diet of rosemary and bramble.

There was another occasion, this time in Austria, when the unexpected happened at a most unexpected time. We were on holiday with a nephew and niece, Peter and Frankie, and were staying at a small hotel on the edge of Lake Attersee, thirty miles east of Salzburg. Arriving there late one evening at the height of the holiday season, we found the few residents and the entire staff thoroughly down in the dumps on account of the weather. Normally one expects a certain amount of sunshine while on holiday, but the season this year had been notable for an almost complete lack of sun, and an abundance of torrential rain. It had rained practically throughout the holiday season, and tourists who had booked in for two weeks, hoping to sizzle in the sun, booked out again after two days.

The level of the lake was causing some consterna-

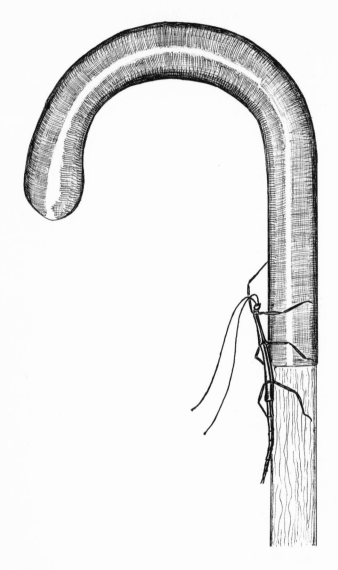

Florida Walking Stick becoming acquainted with an English walking stick.

tion, too. The hotel was situated about twenty yards from the edge of it, and a terrace extended to within ten yards. In a normal season it was the custom for guests to partake of their evening meal on the terrace, and the tables with their checkered coverings and the gaily colored beach umbrellas added a touch of cheerfulness to the scene. This year, however, the tables were bare, and the umbrellas sodden. On the evening of our arrival the level of the lake was only three inches below the level of the terrace; and it was still rising.

From the point of view of collecting insects and reptiles, conditions were not exactly bright. The surrounding countryside would be horribly wet and muddy, and that would mean rubber boots, which was a nuisance because we didn't have any. The chances of finding very many insects or reptiles were pretty slim in any case; in the main they are sun-loving creatures, very much like us, so when the weather is as gloomy and depressing as it was at this period, sensible insects are inclined to seek shelter and more or less disappear from view, again rather like us. We were a trifle dismayed, and went to bed in low spirits. However, being of a highly optimistic nature, we concluded that the sun would positively shine at its most brilliant the next day.

It didn't. When we woke up the next morning it wasn't even visible. Neither was the terrace. The sun was obscured by clouds which extended from east to west and north to south; the terrace was obscured by the lake which extended right across it, having risen alarmingly during the night. The water was now almost up to the level of the one low step which led into the hotel itself. The few disconsolate residents who occupied the ground-floor rooms removed their belongings fast when they saw the lake lapping around the doorway, and took themselves up to the first floor. As for the terrace, it looked a forlorn sight indeed with the tables and chairs paddling in the lake, and the cat's meat floating about in a bowl, bobbing in and out among the table legs. We wondered if the cat was also floating about.

The lake continued to rise during the day, as everyone expected, and by lunchtime had reached the top of the step and was flowing merrily into the lounge, through the hall, and into the kitchen where the cook was awash, ankle-deep in water, frying sausages and *Wienerschnitzel*. Our prospects for collecting anything that day were distinctly dim. But the unexpected happened.

For want of anything else to do, we had wandered downstairs to the terrace with Peter and Frankie, and were paddling about discussing what on earth we could do all day. Peter, an undergraduate at Oxford, and a keen biologist, spied something resembling a grasshopper wriggling about on the surface of the water, under one of the tables. He tried to capture it by cupping his hands beneath it and lifting it clear of the water, but it cascaded over his fingers at every attempt. Frankie, always full of bright ideas, disappeared into the kitchen and returned with a vegetable strainer. This did the trick; it was immersed in the water and lifted clear again under the creature. As it did so, the water poured out but the wriggling animal remained in, waterlogged but safe in the bottom of the vegetable strainer.

We examined it in its very bedraggled state. It was about two inches long, and the front part of its body was covered in some sort of shield, rather like armor plating. The front pair of legs was considerably stouter and stronger-looking than the remaining legs, and we strongly suspected the insect to be of the burrowing type. On this assumption, we placed it in one of our plastic boxes, providing it with a deep layer of earth and a handful of grass. Not knowing for certain what it was, we didn't know for certain what it ate, but we gave it a wide choice of refreshments in the shape of fruit, egg, meat, fish, and vegetables, and left it in peace to dry out in the warmth of the kitchen, and with the comforting whiff of fried *Wienerschnitzel* to give it an appetite.

Apart from this unidentified object, a few spiders which we found in the attic and which surrendered without a murmur, and a frog which had swum gaily into the lounge and taken up residence in the waste-paper basket, we had nothing else of interest to bring back to the Zoo. A disappointingly small and not very interesting catch, we thought. But the unidentified object turned out to be something which the Zoo had not had for a very long time: a mole cricket. It was reported in the evening papers as being comparatively rare and seldom seen, owing to its subterranean habits; for this same reason it was not often seen by the public once it had arrived at the Zoo, for it lived underground most of the time in its cage. But it went on display at the annual show of the Amateur Entomologists' Society, and became an object of interest.

Had it not rained during those holidays in Austria, the Zoo would not have acquired this interesting creature. It must have been washed from its underground home and brought down to the lake by the flood waters; by good fortune it put in an appearance on the terrace at the same moment that we were paddling there, and was duly rescued. One reads in the newspapers about people being rescued from flood waters; it is quite a change to read about the rescue of a mole cricket.

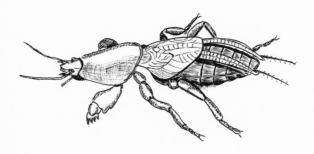

14: 👥 A Frog in the Lounge

Another rather amusing incident happened while we were waiting at Nassau Airport for our plane. Again, we were on our way back to England laden with a variety of livestock. We had completed the first part of our trip from Florida to Nassau without incident, and had several hours to wait before the night plane was due to leave. This gave us time to do some bird watching in the vicinity of the airport, and we were delighted to see several species which are not found in Florida. There were Stripe-headed Tanagers, Bananaquits, and a hummingbird known as the Bahama Woodstar. We also saw some rather attractive lizards but they scampered away swiftly before we were able to get within reach. They would have made a welcome addition to our collection.

Early in the afternoon it began to rain, which put an

end to our search for new birds, and we were forced to retire to the airport lounge. It rained heavily and did not stop until well after dark. However, even the rain brought its benefits in the shape of frogs, and from where we were sitting in the lounge we could plainly hear them croaking outside. We glanced at one another, each with the same thought; we looked at the clock and wondered whether there would be time to go on a short frog hunt before our plane departed. Just

then came an announcement over the loud-speakers;
the authorities regretted to state that owing to the bad
weather the night flight to London would be delayed
by an hour and a half, and would now depart at 10:30
P.M. As far as we were concerned, this was excellent
news and we rejoiced over the delay, though the
remaining eighty passengers felt differently about it.
None of them had the slightest desire to catch frogs,
and they were justifiably annoyed at having an extra
hour and a half to wait.

We made for the central doorway leading out of the
airport and stood on the edge of the parking field
listening to the sound of croaking which emanated
from numerous puddles around. We selected one particularly rich, deep-throated croak from just beyond
the taxi stand, and strolled over to investigate. A puddle
gleamed romantically under a lamp post and there,
right in its very middle, sat a charming little frog croaking away as though it was ready to burst. It was difficult
to discern its markings in the dim light of the lamp post,
so we were unable to see if it belonged to the same
variety of frog which we had already captured in
Florida; since we were now in Nassau, however, we
hoped that it would be of a different kind. We quietly
took up our positions, one on either side of the puddle,
and moved closer in; a sudden splash, a quick grab,
one final astonished croak, and the frog found itself
firmly gripped by a hand which unceremoniously thrust
it deep into a trouser pocket.

Returning to the crowded lounge, we strolled over
in a casual and leisurely fashion to the corner where we
had previously placed our traveling bags, wondering
what people would think if the frog should let forth an

urgent and despairing croak from the depths of a trouser pocket. Fortunately it behaved itself and remained silent; it was probably too startled to croak, anyway. Now came the problem of transferring it from its temporary accommodation in a pocket to a more permanent home in a plastic box. Obviously it was desirable to carry out the transfer without attracting the attention of the other passengers; on the other hand, several of them had made themselves exceedingly comfortable in armchairs which were only a few yards from our baggage, and facing it.

In the confined space of an airport lounge, where people have virtually nothing to do except await announcements, it is extraordinary how the slightest and most trivial happenings become events of some importance. It was quite evident that our mere arrival in the corner was of absorbing interest to a number of people sitting nearby. We hadn't the slightest doubt that we were being looked at, compared with one another, and discussed in whispering tones as to whether or not we were twins. That did not bother us in the least; we were far more concerned with the possibility of the frog attracting even more attention than our twinnishness.

Meanwhile, the frog was beginning to squirm and it seemed likely that it was planning to leap to freedom. We had to act quickly, regardless of any spectators; at the same time, we had no wish to disclose the fact that our four traveling bags were all practically full up with plastic boxes, each one containing something alive. Quietly humming the opening bars of Beethoven's Violin Concerto in D major, one of us opened the zipper on the bag farthest away from the armchairs and extracted an empty plastic box. The other one, whistling a fragment from Mozart, withdrew the frog from its hiding place and proceeded to pop it into the plastic box. The frog, however, proceeded to pop out again before the lid was securely on, and in two gigantic leaps landed on the knee of an elderly lady sitting comfortably in one of the armchairs.

The lady, with admirable composure, remarked, "Oh! A frog!" This was a perfectly sane and sound observation to make since there was, in fact, a frog perched upon her knee and looking even more astonished at its unfamiliar surroundings than the lady who owned the knee. Nevertheless, a pronouncement of that nature was a trifle out of the ordinary, coming as it did from a lady sitting in an airport lounge, and a dozen heads turned to look first at the lady and then at the frog. Eyebrows were raised when one of us dived at the frog, grabbed it by a leg, and bundled it quickly into the box, slamming the lid on firmly. The eyebrows went higher still when we opened the traveling bag in order to replace the plastic box, and thereby revealed a number of similar boxes which were precisely what we had hoped to conceal. Question marks appeared on the faces of the onlookers. Did all our boxes contain frogs? And what about the other three traveling bags standing in the corner; were they full of frogs, too? Beethoven's Concerto descended rapidly from D major into B flat while we fumbled to do up the zipper of the traveling bag. Fortunately, at this highly critical moment, another announcement came over the loud-speakers which distracted the attention of the passengers just long enough for us to close the bag and retreat to the refreshment counter for something soothing.

It was perhaps inevitable that when we climbed the steps leading up to our plane about an hour later, the lady who was so recently associated with the frog should happen to be immediately behind us. We felt that she had deliberately maneuvered herself into this position, in order to question us about it.

She had. Halfway up the steps she tapped one of us on the shoulder.

"Do excuse me," she began, "but did you *really* put that frog into your baggage? And won't it suffocate?"

"Oh no," we replied, anxious to terminate our acquaintance before it even began, "it will be all right there."

"But *why* did you put it in?"

"Well, we are schoolmasters, you see," we explained, our thoughts racing on to keep ahead of our words, "and we thought a Nassau frog would be most interesting to show during a Nature Study period."

By now we were at the top of the steps entering the aircraft; a stewardess looked at our tickets and conducted us to our seats at the rear of the plane. We turned around to see if the lady was likely to sit anywhere near us, and were delighted to see her being conducted to her seat right at the front of the plane.

The last we saw of her was after we had disembarked at London Airport. We were at the Customs counter and our four bags of livestock had gone straight through without even being looked at. But she was having trouble over an undeclared bottle of perfume and several pairs of nylon stockings.

15: Next Stop—the African Forest

To celebrate our fiftieth birthday, we decided to do a collecting trip in a really tropical and jungly part of the world. Bending over our maps, we quickly discovered that the nearest piece of jungle to London was in West Africa. The next step was to find out whether we had any obscure relatives living out there. In spite of exhaustive inquiries, we were unable to trace either kith or kin upon whom we could descend. But Edward, our elder brother, knew of a Mr. and Mrs. Day who lived in Ghana, and promised to look up their address. It turned out that Mr. Day was a professor of something at the University of Ghana, and his wife was a doctor at the local hospital. After a few polite letters to and fro, we invited ourselves to stay with them for a couple of weeks.

During our preliminary planning, we made a list of

the various creatures which the Zoo particularly
wanted. Topping the insect parade was a beetle, one of
the largest beetles in the world: the Rhinoceros
Beetle. It has a large, bulky body and two enormous
curved horns projecting forward from the head—
altogether a solid-looking affair, fearsome and mon-
strous in appearance but quite harmless in reality. We
felt that half a dozen of these frightful creatures
would make a most exciting display in the Zoo's Insect
House. Second in the hit parade was the Imperial Scorpion. Of all the many varieties of scorpions found all
over the world, the Imperial happens to be the largest
of the lot, and is found in West Africa, including
Ghana. We had already had plenty of scorpion-catching
experience during previous trips to Morocco and
Florida, so we were reasonably confident of capturing
a few Imperials. Other insects on the shopping list
included giant grasshoppers, millipedes half-a-foot
long, spiders in assorted sizes, and several varieties of
Praying Mantis.

As far as reptiles were concerned, the Royal Python
topped the wanted list. This was eminently satisfactory

from our point of view, since Royal Pythons are of
manageable size, reaching somewhere around four feet
or so; other varieties of python go to twenty feet and
beyond, and twenty feet of snake would undoubtedly
present problems. We were, after all, going to stay
with friends whom we had never met; and Mrs. Day
might be a lady who disliked twenty-foot snakes. Even
twenty-inch specimens manage to glue some ladies to
the spot. So we would be perfectly content with a
modest Royal Python or two.

The day of departure came, and we boarded the
plane at London Airport. The nine-hour flight to
Accra was wholly uneventful and we landed at
Accra Airport that evening in the middle of a magnificent sunset. The Customs were a little alarmed and
somewhat suspicious when they inspected our baggage
and found that it consisted almost entirely of empty
plastic boxes. Superior officers were sent for, and we
had to explain the purpose of our trip before we were
allowed through. We then met Mr. and Mrs. Day who
had thoughtfully driven up to the airport to meet us.
Fifteen minutes later, we were all sitting in long, comfortable armchairs sipping long, comfortable drinks;
we also met the only other member of the family,
Johnny, who, at eight years old, promptly offered his
services as guide around that part of Africa.

Early the next morning, Johnny guided us to our
very first capture in the grounds of the University—a
colony of brilliant red spidery-looking creatures which
we saw scurrying about on the ground. They looked
like small blobs of red velvet as we picked up about a
dozen and placed them in a plastic box.

"I wonder what they are and what we should feed

them on," one of us remarked, watching them explore their new and unfamiliar surroundings. Johnny provided the answer by leading us to the home of another professor who was in the Zoology Department of the University.

"Mites," he replied, giving the contents of the box a casual glance. "They're quite common around here, especially after rain. Feed them on paper—tissue paper if possible; they'll thrive."

We gave them pieces of tissue paper in various colors and, much to our surprise, they throve.

We met several other professors and lecturers during the course of the next day or two. Indeed, the whole staff of the University appeared highly interested in our activities, and most anxious to help. Dr. Jago, also of the Zoology Department, was an entomologist and specialized in grasshoppers. One day he offered to take us out in his car to a patch of forest where we might find a certain variety of grasshopper. "As far as I know," he told us, "it is found only in that area and nowhere else in the world."

"How far away is it?" we inquired.

"Oh, about sixty miles," he replied, casually; "no distance at all. I'll pick you up in half an hour." He went into his house to collect a long-handled net and a few small jars. We returned to our house to collect some plastic boxes and a few large sandwiches. Sixty miles might be no distance at all compared with the length and breadth of Africa, but to us, sixty miles meant a picnic. And a picnic in the jungle was our idea of heaven.

Half an hour later we were speeding heavenward across the Accra Plains. After a few miles, the bush-

covered country gradually gave way to forest, and Dr.
Jago slowed down a little so that we could do a spot of
bird watching on the way. We recognized hornbills,
bee eaters and weaver birds, but many of the birds we
saw were unidentifiable.

In due course, we reached the particular patch of
forest where Dr. Jago hoped to find his grasshopper.
He parked the car in the shade of a huge tree growing
by the roadside, and we climbed out. It was unbeliev-
ably hot standing on the road with the sun streaming
down upon our unprotected heads, but as soon as we
stepped off the road and into the dark interior of the
forest, it was delightfully cool—almost cold, in fact.
Nevertheless, the humidity was high enough to cause
perspiration to drip off us with every step.

Before we had been five minutes in the forest, Dr.
Jago gave a shout of triumph. "Here's one!" he cried
out, giving a mighty sweep with his net. We gathered
around to have a look at his capture. It was, to our
inexperienced eyes, a perfectly ordinary browny-greeny
grasshopper and looked just about the same as any
grasshopper in Hyde Park. "You see those two red
dots?" Dr. Jago explained, holding the insect gently
between thumb and forefinger so that we could see
the red markings. "That is what distinguishes this
species from all others, and it has never been found
anywhere else in the world except in this particular
area. Remarkable, isn't it?"

We looked impressed and agreed that it was, indeed,
remarkable; and, between ourselves, we considered it
even more remarkable that anybody should want to
travel sixty miles just to see a grasshopper with two
red dots. But then Dr. Jago was not just an entomolo-

gist; he was a grasshopperyologist and probably one of the leading authorities in all Africa on this insect. His own collection consisted of several hundred species, all laid out in neat rows in glass-topped drawers, and all correctly labeled in Latin.

It was a pity the Zoo did not require any moths or butterflies. There were literally thousands everywhere, mostly resting on plants close to the ground; every single step we took disturbed a dozen or two, and one single sweep of the net would have produced a collection varied enough to keep a schoolboy happily occupied for life sorting them out. Dr. Jago did capture one or two varieties which he particularly wanted, but we were content simply to admire them and wonder why Nature lavished so much beauty in such remote areas. Millipedes, too, were fairly common, though nobody would credit them with very much beauty. Millipedes were on our wanted list, but we refrained from collecting any on this occasion as we were reasonably sure of being able to find all we wanted during our last few days; they would then be nice and fresh when we took them home.

After an hour or two in the forest, we returned to the car and Dr. Jago produced a large flask of ice-cold drinks and sandwiches; we had our own sandwiches and so we dined on the roadside at the edge of the jungle. And then an incredible stroke of luck came our way. While we were elegantly nibbling our sandwiches, another grasshopper chose that particular moment to launch itself into the air and fly right over the car. Dr. Jago saw it and dropped his sandwich with surprise. He grabbed his net and raced after the grasshopper which had landed among some herbage on

A Giant Millipede is captured

the other side of the road. The net swooped and the insect was caught. Nothing very extraordinary about that; Dr. Jago had caught hundreds, probably thousands, of grasshoppers under similar circumstances. What was extraordinary was that this particular grasshopper should have chosen that precise moment to fly across the road at the exact spot, because it was a species of grasshopper which even Dr. Jago had never seen before. He was absolutely elated with his good fortune, and we were too, since we knew exactly how he felt. We would have been equally elated if we had found, say, a Royal Python.

The very next day, we found a Royal Python, right

in the grounds of the University itself. We happened to be sitting with members of the staff in the Zoology Department when an African laborer came running up saying, "Snake, sir, big snake over thar!" He pointed to a rough area of ground between the Zoology Department and the building which housed the Physics Department about two hundred yards away. Hatless, coatless and, in one case, shirtless, we all rushed off, led by the African, until he stopped by a large anthill, at the foot of which was a deep hole in the ground. Borrowing a spade from some laborers nearby, we enlarged the hole until it was big enough to see down into its depths. Meanwhile, Mr. Barry Hughes, one of the lecturers in the Zoology Department, arrived on the scene with a sack, by which time a small portion of snake was visible at the bottom of the hole. As soon as the hole was large enough, one of us donned a glove, delved into the depths, and grabbed a sufficiently large handful of snake to be able to withdraw it carefully from its hiding place. Out came a beautiful, shiny four-foot Royal Python which immediately rolled itself into a ball, head in center, and pretended it wasn't there. We placed it reverently in the sack, gave the African laborer a tip, and walked back to the cool interior of the Zoology Department.

It was our turn to be elated, although we had been more or less in that state ever since setting foot on African soil. But we now had our first real capture, and one of the main items on our shopping list. The Zoology Department offered to look after the snake for us, since they had all the facilities for doing so. We gladly accepted their offer and handed over the python to Barry Hughes who was the snake expert. The reptile went into a large glass-fronted cage, and we went into raptures all the way home.

Having already traveled sixty miles to see a grasshopper, we were not altogether surprised when, a few days later, Dr. Grimes of the Physics Department asked us if we would care to accompany him to a place about a hundred miles away to see a bird.

"It is Picathartes, or Bare-Headed Rock Fowl; very rare indeed," he added in a quite unnecessary attempt to arouse our enthusiasm. "Feel like coming?"

We had no hesitation whatsoever in accepting this second offer to visit heaven, and it was agreed that we should set off at 5 A.M. the next day in order to do the whole journey in the cool hours of early morning. Once again, sandwiches and drinks were prepared. While the primary object of the trip was to see Picathartes, which few white people had ever seen in the wild, we decided that it would also offer a glorious opportunity to do some collecting, since the last three miles of the journey would be on foot through the forest. We had only a vague idea as to what we might find, so we prepared a large selection of plastic boxes of all shapes and sizes, and hoped that they would all contain tenants before we returned home in the evening.

It was still dark when we set off the next morning, and not merely cool but downright chilly. However, Dr. Grimes assured us that we would be dripping by the time we reached our final destination.

"How do you know exactly where to find Picathartes?" we inquired, wondering whether we might be going on a hundred-mile journey for nothing.

"They are nesting there under a huge rock," replied

Dr. Grimes. "I've been going there every week to keep a record of their breeding. There are eleven nests altogether, some with eggs and some without; I'm hoping this week some of the eggs may have hatched."

After an hour's driving, dawn broke and we saw that the road ran through patches of forest, with small, untidy villages strung along the roadside at intervals. As on the previous occasion with Dr. Jago, we slowed down in suitable places to do a spot of bird watching, and stopped in the middle of one particularly thick stretch of forest when some hornbills flew across the road. We got out of the car and walked along the road until we found the hornbills sitting on the branches of a tall, bare tree some thirty yards away.

Dr. Grimes studied them through his binoculars. "Crested Hornbills," he announced after a few moments. "You can plainly see that bushy sort of crest on their heads; it makes them easy to identify and to distinguish from other varieties of hornbill."

We watched the hornbills for a short while, then transferred our gaze to various other birds which moved about the thick green foliage. We knew some of them, though the majority were unknown to us. While we were looking through our binoculars at one particular bright red bird, it flew into a small bush growing by the roadside; we gazed at the bush, fascinated, not because of the bird which had disappeared into its interior, but because of a huge cobweb which stretched from the bush to a tree a few paces away. It was not an ordinary, everyday sort of cobweb, but the most beautiful golden color which shimmered in the sun with every breath of wind. And right in the center sat the queen of all spiders. She was the size of a large grape and dressed in a brilliant yellow coat with startling black lines around the waist and hem. Her eight long legs stretched out delicately in eight different directions as she sat in the middle of her kingdom looking regal and elegant.

We went into ecstasies of delight as we stood there gazing at this gem. Then we went into action, determined that this magnificent creature should be captured unharmed. We selected the very largest of our plastic boxes and advanced slowly upon the spider. She remained upon her throne quite motionless and permitted one of us to hold the empty box on one side of the web and the lid on the other side, then slowly bring the two together, with her Majesty in between. She was too regal to struggle; only when the lid was firmly on the box and we had to tear away the central portion of the web did she show any signs of alarm. But it was too late; the spider was in the middle of the web, and the middle of the web was safely in the plastic box. We carried her carefully back to the car and, rather than place the box on the floor where it might be shaken about, we treasured it on our knees for the rest of the journey.

After another half-hour's drive, we arrived at a small village which marked the end of the road. Parking the car under a tree, we gathered our collecting equipment, made sure the spider was comfortable, then set forth on foot along a narrow path leading into the forest. By now, the sun was well up and Dr. Grimes was absolutely correct. We dripped. And we were only at the beginning of a three-mile trek along the rapidly worsening path. We walked in complete silence and in single file, Dr. Grimes leading and pausing occasionally to negotiate a fallen tree or clamber down a deep ravine. After about an hour and a half, we came to what appeared to be a huge cave, formed by a massive rock overhanging the path. Dr. Grimes stopped, unhooked his haversack, and took a few gulps from his water bottle. We did likewise. He then pointed to the roof of the cave, which was about twelve feet high.

"Those are the nests," he said, pointing them out one by one, "and we'll be able to see inside them as soon as I've fixed this mirror." He withdrew a small shaving mirror from his haversack and fixed it on the end of a long pole leaning against the wall of the cave. We then noticed numbers chalked on the rocky floor of the cave, each number directly beneath each nest. In this way, Dr. Grimes was able to record the progress of each nest and its contents. With the mirror tied on the end of the pole, he raised it until the reflection of the nest's interior could be seen. Two nests contained

G.A.G.

eggs; two more contained young birds; and the remainder were empty. Dr. Grimes made innumerable notes in a book while we kept a watch for the parent birds which, quite obviously, were not far away.

We sat quietly in convenient, though not very comfortable, positions and waited in silence. In watching for birds, the essential thing is not so much to keep out of sight as to remain still and as quiet as possible. After about ten minutes, our patience was rewarded; a Picathartes flew down from a tree and hopped onto a low branch just outside the cave. We slowly raised our binoculars to obtain a better view, when another one came and perched on the same branch; obviously the wife. They were evidently suspicious of our presence, however, and after a few moments flew off out of sight. Brief though it was, we had nevertheless had a very clear view of the birds. Having no wish to disturb them any longer, we arose from our cramped positions, took another gulp from our water bottles and started back along the path.

This time we went at a leisurely pace, stopping at frequent intervals to probe under the bark of trees, or lift up rotten logs in our search for specimens. We found a number of eight-inch-long millipedes, three frogs of unknown kind, and a variety of beetles, all of which went into plastic boxes. By the time we reached the village, twenty-two of our boxes were occupied. The black-and-yellow spider was still safely in its container, so we caught a fly and gave it to her for lunch. We then sat down by the side of the car and had our own lunch, watched with curiosity by hordes of wide-eyed children. Dr. Grimes had brought a box of cube sugar, but as soon as it was opened, about two dozen small black hands appeared and, within seconds, the sugar had disappeared.

The return journey by road was also done at a leisurely pace, and we kept our eyes open for any more golden cobwebs. We were lucky; we spotted three more, all quite near the place where we had found the original one. They were every bit as magnificent as the first, and we captured all three of them. What a display these four gems would make back in the London Zoo! Meanwhile, we had to devise means of keeping them alive until we returned to London.

That night, we went to bed utterly worn out; it had been our most exciting and successful day so far and we had enjoyed every minute. We gave our four spiders the most comfortable quarters we could find, much to the horror and dismay of Mrs. Day who shuddered every time she saw even the tiniest of spiders. But Mrs. Day was of the shuddering type, like our sister Edna who came with us on our very first trip to Morocco. No doubt it is quite proper and ladylike to shudder at spiders, but Mrs. Day went a step further; she locked her bedroom door. She didn't in the least mind lions, or buffalo, or even crocodiles, but she just couldn't abide spiders.

Meanwhile, we went to sleep with our treasures on a shelf three feet above our heads, and with a funny feeling that we would not be invited to stay with the Days again.

16:  Beetles That Go Bump in the Night

We were having tea on the terrace. Mrs. Day had invited some friends for tea, and we all sat in comfortable chairs, sipping tea and chatting idly about this and that. The ladies had arranged themselves in decorative groups around the terrace, while Mr. Day, a perfect host if ever there was one, poured the tea and passed the sandwiches. Mrs. Day entertained her guests charmingly, and Johnny amused himself between cakes by building a castle with our empty plastic boxes. We generally made sure that some plastic boxes were within easy reach, even at a tea party on the terrace.

We sat together and discussed in low tones how quickly we could leave the party without appearing too impolite. To us, tea parties are affairs which should be endured only as long as the cakes last. When the final cake vanishes, we like to vanish too and get on with something a little more exciting. However, on this occasion it was the ladies who vanished first, simultaneously and with a rapidity seldom experienced at tea parties.

Mrs. Day had been naming some of the rare and beautiful flowers which graced her garden. Flowers can usually be relied upon to provide a favorite topic of conversation among ladies at tea parties. So can fashions. Fashions had not yet been mentioned, but would undoubtedly have been the next item to discuss if *IT* hadn't appeared on the scene. *IT* was a scorpion, an Imperial Scorpion, fully six inches in length, and black, shiny, and menacing as it slowly emerged from one of the flower beds, walked across the terrace, and stopped only an inch away from the chicken sandwiches. The conversation ended in mid-air as everybody's eyes were riveted on the horror now in our midst; but only for a moment. In magnificent harmony, the ladies shrieked in alarm as they rose in a body from their seats and charged into the house. We uttered a joint yell of triumph and reached for the nearest plastic box. Johnny went up a tree. Only Mr. Day remained completely unruffled as he leaned forward from his chair, gazed for a moment at the scorpion, and then helped himself to another cake. The only precaution he took was to raise his feet onto one of the empty chairs so recently vacated by the departing ladies.

We simply did the necessary, which was to place a plastic box over the scorpion, slide a folded newspaper under it, turn the whole thing upside down, and replace the newspaper with the lid. The scorpion was now a prisoner inside the box, furious at being trapped so easily. The all-clear signal was given, and the ladies reappeared and sat down rather nervously on the edge of their chairs, ready to vanish again at a moment's notice. Conversation was resumed, and the horrors of darkest Africa were discussed in hushed whispers.

We of course were delighted. Not only had we captured our first Imperial Scorpion, but we now had a first-class excuse to leave the gathering. We assured the ladies that we would prowl around the garden and make quite certain there were no more scorpions lurking in the undergrowth. And it was in the undergrowth that we promptly found another one. Fortunately it was behind some bushes, and we were able to capture it without the ladies' even being aware of its existence. We didn't want to give the impression that our home was shared by vast numbers of scorpions.

In due course the ladies departed, still a little shaken but obviously relieved to know that the horror was safe in its plastic box. In the course of the next few days several of the neighbors brought us a variety of creatures caught in their gardens or in the nearby bush. A number of praying mantises arrived in jam jars, a couple of beetles were deposited on the doorstep in a biscuit tin, and a chameleon was brought along in a hat. The owner of the hat was an African houseboy who claimed that the chameleon was extremely poisonous and he had risked his life in bringing it to us. Furthermore, his hat was now contaminated and he could never wear it again. Most Africans hold that a chameleon is evil and should be killed. Chameleons, in fact, are completely harmless, and indeed perform a great deal of good by eating up a number of pests. However, the African was convinced that his days were numbered and his hat useless, so we comforted him by offering him a shirt of many colors. This he put on immediately since he had arrived shirtless as well as hatless. The chameleon, meanwhile, was put in a nearby tree where it went to sleep.

The next scorpion that came our way was found by a 14-year-old boy named Robert who lived in a house not far away. To be more accurate, Robert was found by the scorpion which promptly stung him on the foot. It is not uncommon for natives to be stung by scorpions. Many African children walk about bare-footed, and many a bare toe has suffered accordingly. Robert's toe was now suffering, and Mrs. Day, being the nearest doctor, received an urgent message by telephone to go immediately to Robert's home. We went too on the off-chance that the scorpion was still around. It was. We found it under a large flat stone where it had hidden itself. It was another Imperial Scorpion looking very pleased with itself at having successfully jabbed another toe. But Robert's toe was the last that this particular scorpion would ever sting. While Mrs. Day dealt with the boy in her customary manner, we dealt with the scorpion in our customary manner, and within a very few moments it found itself inside a plastic box and out of harm's way. It was evident that scorpions were comparatively common around the inhabited areas, and indeed we found several more before we left the neighborhood.

We had four days left of our holiday, and although
we had quite a satisfactory collection of creatures, we
still had no Rhinoceros Beetles. However, we
intended spending one night in a rest-house situated
in an area of forest some fifty miles distant, and we
were assured by people who had been there that we
would certainly find Rhinoceros Beetles there.

Meanwhile, we went fishing. Not the normal sort of
fishing where one sits for hours on the banks of a
stream just waiting for a fish to be hooked. Our fish
were not that sort of fish at all. We were after mudskippers. Now mudskippers are very remarkable fish in
that they spend a great deal of their time out of water,
sitting on the muddy banks of lagoons, or resting on
branches sticking out of the water. They are not very
large, as fish go, mostly about five or six inches; but

they are very wary, and with their bulging eyes situated on top of their heads they quickly spot trouble approaching and disappear in a flash beneath the water. The Curator of the Zoo Aquarium had asked us to catch some if possible and send them by air to the Zoo, and, always anxious to oblige, we made preparations.

The University supplied us with a van, some nets, and a couple of native boys who knew considerably more than we did about the peculiarities of mudskippers. The Zoo had already provided us with a specially constructed tin box large enough to hold two or three dozen specimens. We called at the airport and made the necessary arrangements there. Finally we set forth for some lagoons near the coast, and began to look for mudskippers. They were not difficult to find; indeed, they seemed to be everywhere. But they were exceedingly difficult to catch. We had only to take a step or two toward them and they would hop smartly across the mud into the water. To add to the difficulties, the mud was soft and squelched each time we set a foot in it, and indeed our feet sank into the ooze. More than once we were stuck in the mud (reminding us of our boyhood days when we were known as stick-in-the-muds), and we spent a considerable time slithering about in the slosh and getting nowhere near a mudskip-

G.A.G.

per. The two natives, however, were more successful; they plunged waist deep into the lagoon and managed to net a few of them. The nets were passed back to us, and we tipped them out gently into the container, thereby convincing ourselves that our presence on the scene was essential.

At one stage we noticed some crabs climbing the mangrove trees at the edge of the lagoon. As long as we were catching tree-climbing fish, we thought we might as well add some tree-climbing crabs to our collection, especially as they were colored rather attractively in pink and black. We extricated ourselves from the ooze, into which we had gone downwards, and made for the trees, into which we went upwards, scrambling after the crabs which climbed higher still into the topmost branches. Fortunately the trees were not very high, and the crabs not very difficult to capture. Eight of them fitted snugly into a large plastic box. We felt well pleased with ourselves, and rejoined the two natives who were still putting a great deal of effort into the task of mudskipper catching. After about two hours we had caught twenty-one, or to be more accurate, the natives had caught twenty, and we had managed somehow to catch one. We gave each of the natives a handful of money and a handsome shirt, then returned to the airport with our cargo of crabs and mudskippers. After signing a few documents, we left them in the care of an official, and one can claim with reasonable certainty that these twenty-one mudskippers and eight crabs had never climbed as high as they did that night when they became airborne. They arrived at the London Zoo early the following morning, all in excellent health.

The day came for us to go to that rest-house in the forest where we hoped to catch some Rhinoceros Beetles. Mr. and Mrs. Day drove us there, together with Johnny, as they knew the people who ran the place. After a pleasant drive, much of it through thick forest, we arrived in time for lunch and, in the middle of a steaming hot day, we were served with a steaming hot curry which apparently is intended to cool one down in some peculiar fashion. We would have chosen a cold chicken salad if we had had a choice, but we had no choice. Curry it had to be, but we washed down each mouthful with a gulp of ice-cold drink.

Shortly after lunch the Days retired for a rest, and we went out to explore the surrounding forest. Gray parrots flew screaming over the treetops, hornbills cackled from their lofty perches, and unknown creatures buzzed and hissed and squeaked and whistled all around us. We were utterly entranced. As usual we carried an assortment of plastic boxes and into these went an assortment of beetles, bugs, centipedes, millipedes, two more scorpions, two more frogs, two more toads, and two more lizards. We felt like a traveling Noah's Ark. There were no signs of any Rhinoceros Beetles, but we had been told they did not emerge until after dark and we would find them buzzing around the lights of the rest-house. So there we returned about teatime and released our newly acquired collection in the bathroom. We have always found bathrooms are excellent places for keeping reptiles and insects as there are invariably many receptacles in which the creatures can exercise themselves. Bathtubs, washbowls, basins, dirty linen baskets, all can become temporary homes, even if it does mean a certain degree

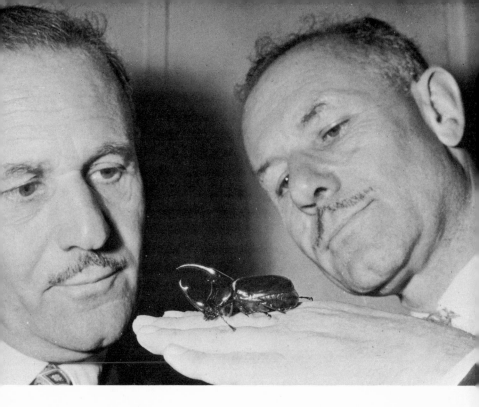

A Rhinoceros Beetle meets the authors

of discomfort as far as we are concerned. In the rest-house all the windows were screened with fine wire-mesh to keep out mosquitoes. This also served the purpose of keeping in the spiders which we liberated in the corners of the bathroom. They proceeded to build cobwebs for themselves before settling down for the night.

At dusk we switched on all the veranda lights to attract any passing Rhinoceros Beetles, and, within minutes, our first beetle had hurtled into the light and fallen to the floor almost at our feet. We grabbed it

A Rhinoceros Beetle meets an obstacle

eagerly, and it looked a most fearsome creature as it struggled to escape from our fingers, and even hissed loudly in its efforts to get away. Into a plastic box it went, soon to be followed by another, and then another. Before we finally went to bed, no less than twenty-nine were hissing in plastic boxes, and another twelve we let loose in our bedroom, much to our sorrow. They flew around all night, banging into walls, furniture, windows, and us. By morning they were exhausted and most of them lay on their backs on the floor. We examined our entire collection of Rhinoceros Beetles, selected the thirty best specimens, and released the others. The manager had looked in once and received something of a shock when one of them landed on his head. These beetles have tiny claws on their feet, and six feet each armed with a set of sharp claws can be quite painful when they are crawling and scratching about on one's bald patch.

When we left the rest-house the next afternoon, we had another funny feeling. The manager had come to wave us good-by, and we felt that never before had he been so delighted to see the backs of his customers.

We left Africa in much the same way as we had arrived—in the middle of a glorious tropical sunset. There was the usual hustle and bustle at the airport, the weighing of luggage, the showing of passports, and one thing and another, but at length we were deemed to be fit and proper persons to travel, and in company with large numbers of other people we eventually boarded our Boeing. Most people normally carry on board a plane a small traveling bag or suitcase, and

perhaps a coat and camera or handbag. When we return from one of our collecting trips, however, we prefer to carry all our livestock with us rather than leave it in the hands of porters and have it eventually confined to the hold. On this occasion we were each carrying two large holdalls bulging with plastic boxes, a string bag also full of boxes, and an assortment of cameras, field glasses, and other bits of equipment dangling about our persons. We also had with us a large metal container full of lizards and boldly marked LIVESTOCK: HANDLE WITH CARE. The air hostess who greeted us at the top of the steps as we entered the plane was too astonished to protest, and merely asked us not to place any luggage on the racks. We have generally been fortunate enough in finding spare seats on the plane, and our luggage has sat very comfortably on seats; but on this trip there wasn't a spare seat available, at least not in the tourist compartment. But we did notice that the first-class compartment was only half-full.

"Plenty of spare seats there," we remarked as we sat in our rather cramped tourist-class seats and tried to find room for our feet. Our baggage occupied all the floor space, and short of sticking our feet up on the shoulders of the passengers in front of us, we would have had to endure several hours of acute discomfort. But the hostess came to our rescue. We hopefully suggested to her that we might be permitted to occupy some of the vacant seats in the first-class compartment.

"I'm afraid that would be impossible," she replied charmingly, "but if you care to move some of your baggage there it would give you a lot more space."

That, we agreed, was an admirable suggestion. And

so it came to pass that while we traveled with a reasonable degree of comfort as tourist-class passengers, all our frogs and beetles and scorpions and spiders enjoyed the utmost comfort in the luxury of the first-class compartment. During the journey we paid frequent visits to our livestock to make sure that all was well, and in the semidarkness of the cabin we were able to sprinkle the snake-bags with water and open some of the plastic boxes to let in a little fresh air. The hostess was clearly intrigued with our comings and goings, and with true feminine perception came to the conclusion that we could only be looking after some kittens.

"I adore kittens," she ventured to remark at some stage of the journey. "If you have any to spare, do let me know."

She would surely have had kittens had she known what our baggage really contained!

17:  A Turtle for a Dollar

There were several reasons why we selected New York State for our next collecting trip. First, Dorothy and Ira, our sister and brother-in-law, live at Lake George, a most attractive spot 200 miles north of New York City and right in the heart of the country. Second, we knew that the North American continent offered varieties of reptiles and amphibians which the London Zoo wanted. A third reason was that Dorothy produced the most heavenly desserts on earth, and as we boarded the plane at London Airport we estimated that we would arrive at Lake George just about in time for dinner.

Our estimation was correct, and Dorothy really excelled herself. The dessert was a dream.

"A cream dream," we echoed by way of congratulation.

"A supreme cream dream," remarked Ira in a tone denoting pure contentment. But this is not intended to be a chapter on how to get fat, so having ensured that Dorothy's cream dreams pass into literary history, we can return to the subject of collecting.

We had two weeks in which to amass whatever we could. The first week would be spent in locating suitable areas where we might find snakes, frogs, toads, salamanders, insects, spiders, and anything else suitable for the Zoo. During this week we also looked around for reinforcements in the shape of schoolboys who were likely to be far more knowledgeable regarding the location of snakes, and far more agile than we could be in their ultimate capture. So our first destination was the neighbors. It is generally a good thing to arouse the interest of the neighbors when one wishes to collect reptiles. It gives them a feeling of satisfaction to know that we propose to rid their neighborhood of snakes and other unwelcome creatures. More important still, it gives us an excuse to trespass in their gardens. Dorothy has only one neighbor, whose garden is separated from her own by a low wooden railing. Both gardens, which covered several acres, were partly lawn, partly cultivated, and partly wooded, and seemed a likely place for snakes desiring a little peace and seclusion.

For reinforcements we enlisted the aid of the Ricketson family. Mr. Ricketson had a car, and we didn't. Mrs. Ricketson could produce sandwiches. Duane Ricketson, 15, was already an experienced snake collector; and his brothers—Zan, a year older, and Bruce, a year younger—were equally enthusiastic. There was another brother, Teddy, but he was only eighteen

A Milk Snake goes into a plastic box

months old and was unlikely to play a major part in the business of catching snakes, unless we used him as bait. The family lived at Warrensburg, some five miles north of Lake George, and Duane had already told us that the country around their home was excellent for snakes.

Through Duane we met Michael Eggleston, a 12-year-old Scout who had never had any snake-catching experience, but who was quite prepared to do his good deed by catching any he found. He soon discovered that we were also interested in frogs, and suggested a visit to his camp.

"There is a lake not far from the camp," he said

eagerly, "and you'll sure find plenty of frogs there. I can ask some of the boys to help catch them."

"How many Scouts are camping with you?" we inquired.

"I guess there are about two hundred," replied Michael, beaming. We beamed too. Two hundred Scouts meant two hundred pairs of hands, and two hundred pairs of hands could conceivably catch two hundred frogs. Not that we wanted them at this stage; a dozen or so would do nicely for the time being.

Mr. Ricketson drove us to the camp the next day, together with Duane and Michael. Camp Wakpominee was beautifully situated in thickly wooded country

On the Schroon River

Frogs in the bathtub

near West Fort Ann. We arrived in time for a good
hearty lunch, and then joined in some of the sing-
songs so beloved by Scouts. But we were more anxious
to join in the chorus of frogs which could be heard
croaking down in the marsh by the lake, and it was not
long before we slipped out and made our way to the
marsh, followed by Michael and Duane and several
more Scouts, including Thomas Ward. Thomas Ward
was Nature Director at Explorer Post 18, and we added
him to our growing army of collectors and made a note
of his telephone number.

Very soon we were all wallowing in the mud, and
the Scouts brought us frogs of every shape and size: big
ones and little ones, brown ones and green ones, lumpy
ones and warty ones. The warty ones of course were

toads, as the Nature Director quickly pointed out. Many of the specimens were leopard frogs handsomely marked and easily identified. One bright green one which Michael had caught leaped from his hand straight into a plastic box. Michael was completely entranced with the part he had played in renewing the frog population of the London Zoo.

We selected a dozen best-quality specimens and returned with them to Lake George. Ira was anything but entranced when he discovered the frogs in his bathtub that evening.

"They are only there temporarily," we explained soothingly.

Ankle-deep in mud at Camp Wakpominee

"And I'm here permanently," replied Ira, planting his feet firmly astride the bath mat as if to emphasize his permanency.

"But you would make such a nice, gently sloping island for the frogs to climb on while you are having a bath," we told him amidst laughter.

Dorothy came to the rescue. "There is a spare bathroom upstairs. Why not take all your frogs and keep them up there?"

It was the perfect solution, and the frogs were transferred at once to the spare bathtub where they indicated their pleasure by croaking all night.

The first week slipped by, and we made notes of areas which we proposed to visit again during the second week. We also visited Animal Land, one of many holiday attractions situated on the road between Lake George and Glens Falls. Here was displayed a number of animals, birds, and reptiles, including snakes and turtles. Many of the reptiles had, in fact, been caught by Duane Ricketson, which accounted for his experience as a snake catcher.

We started collecting in earnest that second week, and went first to Glens Falls where we contacted Thomas Ward again, his brothers—Timothy, 16, and Jonathan, 14—and a friend of theirs, James Comstock, 14, assistant Patrol Leader of Troop 444. These four boys, all students at South Glens Falls High School, volunteered to take us to the woods bordering the Hudson River, and in these woods and along the banks of the river we spent many fruitful hours turning over rocks and logs and digging among the undergrowth, much to the surprise of a few sleepy fishermen nodding away peacefully by their lines. It was James who came up with the first capture: a salamander. Until now we had not bothered too much with newts and salamanders as they are not easy to keep, and most of those we had seen were too small anyway. True, they might have made an appetizing morsel for some of our snakes, but we didn't have the heart to use them as food. However, the specimen found by James was reasonably large, so we kept it. Before long we had another five.

In the meantime Thomas and his brothers had waded into the Hudson River in the hope of disturbing a turtle. We wanted a turtle or two, but only very small ones. Turtles are somewhat weighty creatures, and a large turtle would certainly have weighed too much and have been slightly awkward to carry. The question of weight has to be considered very carefully; we carry our livestock with us on the plane, and our baggage allowance is strictly limited, as it is with all passengers. Once upon a time, when we were small and grubby, our schoolteacher endeavored to drum into our heads certain facts about certain weights: 16 ozs. = 1 lb., 14 lbs. = 1 stone, and so on. (There were more weights to be learned, but we never got any further.) On our collecting trips, however, we made up our own table of weights which went something like this: 10 frogs = 1 snake, 8 snakes = 1 turtle, 2 turtles = 1 pair of shoes, 6 turtles = 1 complete suitcase. So we had to rule out all but the smallest turtles, and the Ward family, wading in the river, looked in vain for small turtles. They didn't show up that day.

But poison ivy did. For the best part of an hour, while the Wards were deep in the river, and James was deep in the woods, we were deep in poison ivy along the river bank. Of course we didn't know it. We had never met the plant before, and never even knew it existed in this part of the world. Red Indians we were prepared for, but not poison ivy. It was fortunate that we were wearing good strong pants and stout leather shoes, as well as rubber overshoes, and a pair of leather gloves on our hands. This was our normal clothing worn mainly as a protection against rattlesnakes and other fearsome creatures, but this time it protected us from the poison ivy as well. At one stage we actually wished we had brought our swimming trunks with us. The river looked invitingly cool and refreshing, and we would have welcomed the chance to plunge in every now and again as an alternative to searching in the undergrowth. One shudders to think what would have happened had we plunged in among the poison ivy wearing only swimming trunks! It was James who told us about it after we had been in it for nearly an hour. He had been in the woods out of sight and had caught a Garter Snake. This he now brought over to show us, but stood on a rock a safe distance away.

"Say, do you guys know poison ivy when you see it?" he called out hoarsely.

"Poison ivy? Never heard of it," one of us remarked casually. "What's it look like?"

"Well," continued James, "just look around. It's all around you. You're standing in it."

We looked around. A carpet of leaves, some green, some red, covered the ground. This, then, was poison ivy, and anyone foolish or ignorant enough to touch it with bare hands or legs was just asking for trouble. It sets up an irritation on the skin, an irritation which spreads quickly unless given medical attention. Even though clothing offers some protection, it is very

His catch is secure in a plastic box

unwise to handle any clothing which has been in contact with the plant. James warned us not to touch our clothes.

"I guess you had better get rid of your pants," he advised.

But we had no intention of parting with our pants and walking home in our undergarments. We removed ourselves from the area of poison ivy and walked to a grassy patch where we proceeded to pluck handfuls of grass and rub it vigorously against our gloves, our pants, and our shoes. This we hoped would remove any fragments of poison ivy left behind on our clothing. We were thankful to have the boys with us to warn us of such hazards.

With this little danger out of the way, we proceeded to examine the Garter Snake. It was quite a small one, only about 18 inches long, but it was our first Garter. We placed it carefully in a plastic box, and continued searching. During the next hour or so we caught three more Garters and a young Milk Snake, beautifully colored in red and white. Quite a nice little collection for a beginning, it was agreed.

With this lot we returned home and crept upstairs stealthily so as not to disturb Ira, who was sitting in his favorite chair watching a game of baseball on television. We saw no reason to let him know we had caught anything at all.

"Hi," he greeted us when we came down again and entered the room.

"Hi," we replied.

"Catch anything?" he asked.

"Nothing very much. How's the ball game?" Our question was designed to stimulate more interest in the game and less in snakes. But our designs were upset by Dorothy walking in from the kitchen.

"Hello," she said gaily, "what did you find? Any snakes?"

"Oh, just a couple," we admitted. "Very small ones, though, and quite harmless." This was more for Ira's benefit than for Dorothy's. But Ira was immersed in the ball game. It is not even certain whether he was aware of the fact that there were snakes in the house. So we left him with the ball game and planned our next trip.

This was to Warrensburg where the Ricketsons lived. According to Duane the area was excellent for snakes, and we needed some more. Michael Eggleston

Where's that turtle? High hopes of a capture

also came with us again, and our first target was an old dilapidated hut. Here we searched in all the corners for spiders. They occupied every nook and cranny, and we collected a number of the fattest ones within reach. Mr. Ashby of the Insect House was always pleased to have foreign spiders in his collection.

Presently a cry of surprise from Michael rang out. "Hey! Look at this spider!"

We crowded around him and saw that he had found a most beautiful black-and-yellow creature, not unlike the enormous spiders we had found the previous year in Ghana.

"Well done, Mike!" we exclaimed, delighted with his find. "We can certainly do with that one."

Turtling

It went carefully into a plastic box together with a leaf from which to dangle if it felt the need. Spiders like to dangle.

The rest of the day was again spent in our customary manner: upturning hundreds of rocks and boulders, wading happily in swamps, and making ourselves thoroughly hot and sticky and downright nasty to look at. Duane found a number of snakes. He seemed to have some uncanny knack of knowing exactly where to look, exactly which stone to look under. On one occasion when he had fished out a snake from its muddy refuge beneath a rock, he went to wipe his hand on a tuft of grass—and found another snake coiled around that very tuft. It was left to Michael, however, the smallest member of our team, to find the largest snake of all. This was a two-and-a-half-foot Milk Snake which tried to disappear down a hole, but was hauled out by the combined efforts of the boys.

So once more, back home at Lake George that evening, we had to smuggle our collection in, tiptoeing upstairs to add the day's bag to our growing assortment of livestock. We now had nineteen snakes writhing and wriggling about in plastic boxes, as well as an unknown number of frogs and spiders and beetles. In fact we had practically everything we had come to collect from North America, except a turtle. Our final effort, then, was to catch a turtle.

Some of the plastic boxes ready for transportation to the London Zoo

Duane had told us that turtles were to be found in the Schroon River which flowed near his home at Warrensburg, and thither we went on our last excursion. This time we had a small army of four boys to help us: Duane, Michael Eggleston who by now refused to be left out of anything, Raymond Matteau, 15, and Michael Milic, 13. By fair means or foul Duane had managed to acquire a very ancient and wobbly boat complete with a pair of oars and two tin cans. The tin cans were an essential part of the equipment; both had to be used constantly for bailing out the water that seeped through in a dozen places.

Somehow we all managed to embark without the whole thing tipping over, though it wobbled alarmingly from side to side. We sat in the middle, Duane and Raymond squeezed themselves into the bows, and the two Michaels stationed themselves in the stern. All four boys had nets, and each was anxious to make the first capture.

In these circumstances we took turns rowing and rowed with extreme caution, slowly, evenly, and with a minimum of movement. This was necessary not only because of the delicate balance we had to maintain throughout the operation, but also because any undue noise or commotion would frighten away any turtles. There were several around, mostly sunning themselves on logs, and mostly too large for us to bother about. We wanted a small one, and it was only a question of waiting for the right size to show itself before we went into action. The plan was simply to glide very slowly and quietly up to its perch on a log, and then gently place a net over and around it.

We proceeded softly down the river, one of us rowing, one bailing, and the boys alert and scanning every log. There were several turtles, but none quite the right size until . . .

"Look, there's one," whispered Raymond, pointing to a log near the riverbank. We looked. Yes, there was one indeed, exactly the right size, basking in the sun and apparently asleep on its log.

Very slowly we steered the boat toward it, barely lifting the oars from the water for fear of making a splash. Two things were uppermost in our minds: not to upset the boat, and not to frighten the turtle—in that order. Duane happened to be in the best position for netting it. He was well accustomed to handling turtles in Animal Land, even huge snapping turtles. We had every faith in him.

The boat moved slowly nearer and nearer the log. We were almost there. Quietly, patiently, Duane reached forward with his net until it was within inches of the turtle.

Then came disaster! An enormous dog suddenly appeared at the edge of the river, recognized Duane as its owner and master, and bounded straight into the water to greet him, barking and splashing joyfully. The turtle, dozing peacefully up to this moment, dropped off its log with astonishment and disappeared below the surface with a plop. Duane, reaching out too far in a desperate effort to catch it, overbalanced and disappeared with a much bigger plop. And the boat, wobbling under the strain with its balance upset, practically turned turtle itself. We managed to save it just in time, but not before quantities of water had flowed in over the side with a gurgling noise. The dog, not satisfied with the damage already done, added to the general confusion by trying to jump in the now waterlogged boat.

Duane appeared a short way down-river, and swam to the bank. It had been a very hot day, and he was perfectly happy to have fallen in. We were all thoroughly soaked as we turned the boat around and headed for shore—turtleless. It seemed likely that all the turtles up and down the river had heard the commotion, for by now there wasn't one in sight. We had failed to catch a turtle. But it wasn't a complete failure. We did, in the end, secure one.

We bought one. Stopping at Animal Land on our way home, we called in, met the Director—and came out with a turtle.

It cost a dollar.

18: Exceptional Young Zoologists

There are a number of clubs and societies in England which exist to further the aims of those people interested in natural history.

The XYZ Club for Exceptional Young Zoologists is open to young people between the ages of nine and eighteen who are interested in animals generally, including fleas. The Club is based on the London Zoo and Whipsnade, and organizes all kinds of activities for its members. Films, lectures, camera safaris, competitions, and bird counts are attended by eager young naturalists, and the Club was featured in a television program in the A to Zoo series.

In the early summer of 1962, we organized the very first collecting expedition undertaken by members of the XYZ Club. A fairly remote part of Surrey was chosen as a suitable location; good beetle country, by

Insect hunters insect hunting

gad, and South Godstone was the starting point. We had anticipated that about fifteen members, or possibly twenty at the most, would turn up. We had not advertised it very widely; a gentle hint here and there would probably produce enough members for this first collecting expedition, and between us we considered we could manage fifteen or twenty quite comfortably. No less than forty-nine, however, turned up, carrying a formidable supply of nets, trowels, plastic boxes and plastic bags, mostly filled with assorted sandwiches and hard-boiled eggs. The sandwiches and eggs would be dealt with in the customary manner, leaving the plastic boxes available for any livestock captured.

With the party came Mr. George Ashby to act as official adviser, and either accept or reject each creature brought to him. It must be realized that the object of the operation was to collect insects for the Insect House at the London Zoo. Without some sort of advice and guidance it was possible that all sorts of unwanted creatures would be caught and placed in containers, and eventually delivered to the Zoo, only to be given to some other animal as extra food. With Mr. Ashby there on the spot, however, it was simply a matter of making a capture, taking it to him, and acting on his expert and professional advice. If he approved of the creature, it would go on display in the Zoo; if he disapproved, the animal would be returned to its own beloved patch of grass or mud.

With these simple instructions in mind, the party began their search, splitting into groups. For our hunting ground we had selected, first, a large pond with a profusion of reeds and water plants growing around the edges. The peace and stillness of the scene was very quickly shattered as numerous nets plunged in and disturbed the mud at the bottom. We hoped none of the children would plunge in. Several boys did take off their shoes and socks and went paddling, and one boy went paddling without taking off his shoes. The girls were slightly more cautious and ventured as far as the water's edge, where two of them became stuck in the mud. The experience, however, would no doubt provide them with subject material next time they were given an essay to write. All kinds of creatures were caught in the nets, popped into plastic boxes, and taken over to Mr. Ashby for inspection, and it soon became apparent that this collecting expedition was

XYZ Club members on a collecting trip near the Black-water Estuary, Essex

going to be highly successful. One of the first captures was an insect badly wanted by Mr. Ashby: a Great Diving Beetle. So from the start he had a broad smile upon his face, and in fact the whole party was in high spirits throughout the day. Nothing seems to attract boys and girls more than a pond, and to be able to participate in the fun of collecting scientifically from a pond, using the correct equipment, receiving professional advice, and knowing that it was all for a set purpose, was to them a magnificent opportunity not to be missed for anything.

From the pond we moved to a wooded area and

gathered in many more insects as well as some frogs, lizards, and snakes. Again one of the early captures was another one on the badly wanted list: a Stag Beetle. The beating tray was used with great success, and all the plastic boxes and bags and containers were filled with an assortment of creeping, crawling, writhing, and wriggling creatures. It was fortunate that a special coach had been hired to bring the party back to London; passengers on public transport might well have had cause to complain and protest had we all trooped onto a bus with our livestock.

Owing to the success of the expedition, another one

A young alligator meets members of the XYZ Club

was organized some three months later, rather more officially and certainly on a more ambitious scale. Miss Sali Suss, in charge of the XYZ Club activities, and Mr. Michael Boorer, Education Officer, did all the hard work of organizing it, as well as announcing in the Club magazine that a second trip was planned for September. The response was immediate; 160 members applied to take part. This was going to be slightly unwieldy, to say the least, but it was also most encouraging to find so many youngsters seriously interested in the business of collecting.

The location for this trip was a stretch of marshy ground bordering the Blackwater estuary, in Essex. A bird observatory in the neighborhood had been declared "out of bounds" and the party had strict instructions to avoid it. We had no intention of disturbing the bird life of the area, though every intention of removing the insect life. So when four coachloads of eager and enthusiastic youngsters descended upon the marshes, all sensible insects in the vicinity descended into their holes and shelters with commendable speed.

Mr. Ashby was unable to come on this trip, but Mr. Michael White, also from the Insect House, came in his place and took over the duties of examining each captured specimen and deciding whether to accept it or reject it.

Meanwhile the population of Bradwell had taken up vantage points along a bank to behold the extraordinary sight of one hundred and sixty bug-hunters bug-hunting in the mire and mush, spread out along a mile of marshy, boggy land bordering the estuary. Mr. White had brought with him several nets and shovels, though hardly enough to supply such an army. Each member, however, had been asked to bring containers, and before long everyone was busy, container ready at hand, groping about in the grass, in the bogs, in the ditches, on the banks, in the pools, and at the water's edge, chasing after vast numbers of elusive creatures, and yelling triumphantly every time a capture was made. For three solid hours we searched, and caught, and searched, and caught. Mr. White was besieged from all sides by ardent collectors, anxious to know whether their captures were on the wanted list or not. He must have felt something like a casting director for some big film production, accepting this actor, rejecting that.

It was estimated that something in the region of one thousand insects and spiders were caught, and in case anyone should wonder whether the entire neighborhood was completely denuded of insects, it must be stated that at least three times as many were released because they were not suitable for display, or because enough of their species had been caught already. In any case it has been estimated that in an acre of country in the south of England there are about one and a quarter million spiders, not to mention insects. Those who fear we are wiping out the insect population can be reassured.

When our collection reached the Insect House that evening, Mr. Ashby took one look at it and sank into a coma. It was some days before everything was sorted out and identified, but in due course the job was done, and the creatures transferred into their new glass-sided homes and put on display. No doubt many of those exceptionally young zoologists who participated in the collecting expeditions will have visited the Insect House, and seen their own exhibits on display; no doubt many will have felt a sense of elation, perhaps a glow of pride, and rightly too. After all, as members of the XYZ Club, they will have taken an active interest in the affairs of their club and played a prominent part in a scientific undertaking; and thoroughly enjoyed themselves in doing so.

19: Nets

It is possible that some readers by now may be considering going off into the wilds to do a spot of collecting themselves, and presenting their catch eventually to a zoo. Some general hints on the equipment necessary for a collecting trip might therefore be helpful at this stage. One point must be borne in mind, however, if the ultimate intention is to present it all to a zoo; the zoo may not want it. Most zoos are limited in space; they would certainly welcome any creature that was comparatively rare, or strikingly beautiful, or even extraordinarily ugly, and large enough to go on display, but they would politely decline the offer of anything as ordinary and humble as a wood louse, or a bee, or a Cabbage White butterfly. All sorts of weird and exciting insects and spiders may be found abroad, especially in tropical and subtropical

D-shaped net

countries, and here the likelihood of a zoo accepting your catch is much greater. You may even find yourself presenting them with a creature they have never had before. It is even possible you may find an insect entirely new to science, and your name will go down in history as well as in Latin.

Most boys and girls and grownups too, outward-bound on a collecting trip, will want to take some sort of a net. A net seems to come to mind almost at once when you think about collecting, and it is all a question of knowing which is the best kind of net to choose and use. There are in fact three main types of nets: sweep nets, water nets, and fly nets.

Sweep nets are used for sweeping close or fairly close to the ground. Many insects rest or feed in long grass, or on plants and shrubs, and a sweep net is best for collecting these. It will come in for some pretty rough wear, so it must be strong; but it must also be light in weight, otherwise you will soon begin to wonder whether you have caught a ship's anchor in the net. The actual net part should consist of a strong muslin bag, about twelve or fifteen inches in diameter at the open end, and fifteen or twenty inches deep, tapering off at the closed end so that the whole thing is shaped rather like a cone. The mouth of the net must be securely attached to a metal rim; and the rim must be firmly attached to a strong wooden or light metal handle. The length of the handle may vary between fifteen inches and three feet; a short handle has the advantage of making the whole thing lighter, but it has the disadvantage of making you bend more; the longer the handle the farther you will be able to reach,

A sweep net in use

A beating tray in use

but the more your arm will ache. These are things you can only decide for yourself. Is it better to use a short handle and suffer from backache, or to use a long handle and suffer from armache?

Another point to remember is that the net should be portable. A few collectors perhaps do the thing in style and set off to their destination by car, but most collectors probably travel by bus, or on a bicycle, or perhaps on their ten toes. A net with several yards of handle is not easily carried on a crowded bus; nor can a long-handled net be fixed very easily on a bicycle;

something is bound to catch somewhere, and you will finish up in a ditch. True, there are some very attractive insects to be found in a ditch, but you don't want to do a three-point landing among them. All these things have to be considered, and all justify some careful thinking.

Using a sweep net is not difficult and may result in an interesting catch of spiders, beetles, grasshoppers, and other creatures. Open fields of long grass, areas of heather or bracken, and roadside banks of wild flowers are the kinds of places where a sweep net may be used

Larvae cage containing locusts

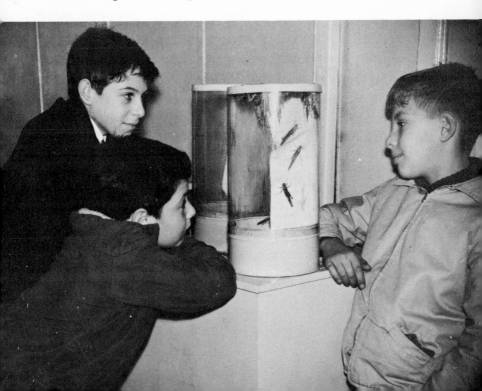

with advantage. The net is held so that the open end
may be waved from side to side through the top of the
vegetation; this movement disturbs any insects shelter-
ing there, and they find themselves in the net. After
about a dozen sweeps the net may be examined, and
any desirable creatures therein may be picked up with
tweezers or fingers and transferred to a suitable container. Further sweeps with the net will produce
further additions to your collection, and you will be
surprised at the number and variety of interesting
specimens that may be caught by this method. Quantities of leaves, small twigs, and other debris will also
be caught up in the net, but you simply extract your
specimens first and throw out the rest. Unwanted creatures, too small or too common to collect, may also be
thrown out with the leaves and twigs. There is no need
to deprive the birds of every living creature.

The water net is not unlike the net small boys use
for catching tiddlers, or the one used for transferring
the goldfish from one tank to another; but it is very
much stronger, very much larger, and very much
better. It must be strong enough to be pushed through
sand or mud at the bottom of a pond, or through reeds
and other aquatic vegetation. The net material must
not only be strong, but must be of a kind that does not
swell in water; otherwise the meshes tend to close up.
This causes the water to bank up in front of the net as
it is swept through the pond, instead of being allowed
to pass through the net. The stout metal ring at the
open end may be round, or triangular, or shaped like
the letter D, and should be roughly ten or twelve
inches across. The net should be firmly attached to the
ring, and the ring firmly attached to a very strong

handle about six feet in length. The handle will have to take the strain of pushing the net through water, so if it is too thin it may soon bend and snap. It is highly annoying to be left with a broken piece of handle in your hand, and the net stuck in the mud at the bottom. You feel very much like a stick-in-the-mud yourself. A round wooden handle about one and a half inches thick would be just about right.

Another calamity that may befall this kind of net is that the net itself may easily be torn on snags hidden in the murky depths of the water. This can be overcome by surrounding the entire net with a heavy canvas bag or apron which is fastened to the metal ring at the mouth of the net. This canvas bag is far more likely to withstand being scraped against rocks and other snags at the bottom of the pond, and it forms a useful protection for the net. Many a choice newt or salamander has managed to escape through a hole in a water net which has not had the protection of a bag around it.

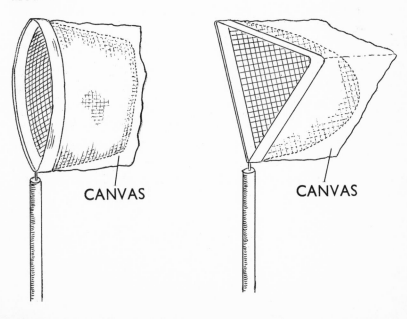

CANVAS   CANVAS

G.A.G.

The water net may be used either from dry land at the edge of a pool or from the middle of the pool if you prefer to wade right in. Don't go in up to your neck, though; people might stare at you, and even dive in to rescue you. With this net you stand a good chance of catching all sorts of water insects as well as newts and frogs and other water-loving creatures. Any specimens you manage to catch and intend to keep should be placed in a container and kept damp until their release into an aquarium. Using a water net can be great fun, provided you don't go home dripping wet yourself.

The third kind of net, the fly net, is the sort so beloved by small boys and elderly professors who use them for chasing butterflies. This net should be made of muslin with a fairly close mesh, and it should be firmly attached to the rim which may be metal, wood, or cane. The ring should be about twelve inches across, and the depth of the net should be twice the width, or even more, tapering towards the closed end so that it is cone-shaped. The ring must be stout, and securely attached to a light but strong handle three or four feet long. A lightweight aluminum handle would be admirable. Remember, you will very likely use this net high in the air, waving it frantically at one solitary insect, swiping at it this way and that, swinging at it mightily and probably missing it anyway. So your net needs to be light; you won't be able to swipe and swing for long if it is too heavy.

Unlike the other two nets, this kind is used mainly for catching one particular insect at a time, and that when it is flying. A moth or a butterfly, fluttering about hither and thither and never making up its mind which way to go, is the favorite target for anyone using a fly net, but a more unusual and exciting target would be a flying beetle hurtling through the air in a most determined fashion. A great deal of skill is necessary to catch one of these insects on the wing, and even when caught the creature will escape unless you are quick. The moment the insect is in the net, you must either bring the net down firmly against a piece of

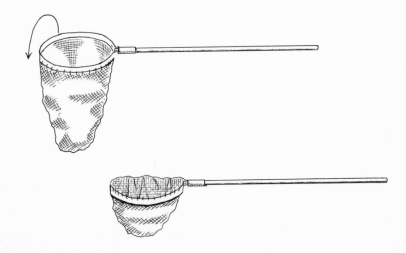

level ground, or else flip the net right over the ring in mid-air, trapping the insect in the folds. That is still not the end of the operation. The insect has to be extracted from the net and placed in a container, and many a beetle has escaped through carelessness on the part of the collector at this critical stage. The safest method is to hold the closed end of the net upwards and allow the insect to fly into the very tip. Then with your hand you can squeeze the net below it, thereby trapping it in a small portion at the end of the net. A jar or container is then placed against the portion being squeezed, and you can then relax your hold, allowing the insect to make one last bid for freedom by flying through the opening and straight into the container.

There is one more kind of net which is worth mentioning, and that is a pocket net. Carried easily in a large pocket or haversack, it might come in very handy on one of those occasions when you are ambling along a country lane, or across the moors, not bent on anything in particular, but just ambling. During your holidays you will not want to go on a collecting trip every moment of every day; there will be other things to do such as swimming, going for walks, or having a picnic. Those are just the occasions when you are likely to spot a brilliantly colored beetle or an enormous spider. It so often happens that these things turn up when you are not prepared for them. Photographers have the same trouble; a scoop, the picture of a lifetime, or the Loch Ness monster presents itself on the one occasion when the camera is left behind. So be on the safe side and always carry a pocket net with you when you go out on a non-collecting trip, even if you are only visiting your grandmother. She is quite likely to have something enormous creeping about at the bottom of the garden.

20: A New Use for an Old Umbrella

Many years ago a gentleman named Mr. Bignell invented a piece of equipment which became known as the Bignell beating tray. In appearance the tray looked something like an open but rather flattened umbrella without a handle, and it could be folded up to make it more easily carried. Its purpose was to help in the collection of insects, and it has been used by generations of insect collectors ever since; it is still a favorite and indispensable piece of equipment with many present-day collectors.

When opened up like an umbrella, it is simply pushed in under a bush or tree; the bush is then tapped smartly with a stick, or shaken by hand, and a host of insects will come tumbling down onto the tray. The very first tap or shake will cause the most insects to drop, for they will have been eating or resting or going about their business quite happily, not in the least expecting to be suddenly jarred from their leaves and twigs. It is the sudden jarring that causes them to lose their grip and tumble. After the first initial shaking they will cling on for dear life, though even then many will not be able to cling on for long.

The beating tray may be bought at shops which deal with this insect-collecting business, but with a little bit of ingenuity something very similar could be made and used for exactly the same purpose. In fact without any ingenuity at all you can use a perfectly ordinary white sheet, or a perfectly ordinary umbrella. You select a suitable tree or bush or more overhanging foliage, and simply spread the sheet out or open up the umbrella under the chosen spot. With an umbrella you could probably stick the point in the ground, or just let the edge of the material come to rest against the leaves. When all is set, tap the foliage above the sheet or umbrella, and the numerous insects will start their plunge. After landing they may remain still for a moment or two, perhaps too astonished and startled to move, or they may feel a trifle embarrassed at their fall from grace and start moving and crawling away under cover. Before they have time to go far, you can pick them up nimbly and pop them into containers.

A slight modification of this method may be used if the foliage is too high to reach with a stick. In this case you can throw a short heavy stick up into the middle of it. A shower of insects may come sailing down upon your head; so might the short heavy stick. So stand back when performing this operation and be ready to leap aside if the stick is coming your way. It is very much the same as knocking down chestnuts.

In some respects a sheet is better than an umbrella. It can be spread over a much larger area; it can be folded up and easily packed away in a haversack; and it can be washed and used over and over again. If a slit is made in the sheet from one edge to the center, then the whole thing can be laid out under a tree, the two sides where it has been split being pulled around either side of the trunk and then closed in again to form an unbroken expanse of sheet, with the tree appearing to grow through the center of it.

One advantage that the umbrella has, however, is that any insects falling into it from the foliage above are likely to slide down to the center and can more easily be seen and captured. Some collectors are perfectly happy to place an umbrella in a suitable position under a tree, tap the foliage overhead, then move the umbrella under a second tree, tap again, and repeat the performance several more times until a large number of struggling insects are gathered in the middle of the umbrella. The collector then closes the umbrella and walks off home with all the creatures tucked away safely inside.

We adopted this method once, but only once. We had collected a nice haul of beetles, spiders, caterpillars, bugs, and other miscellaneous livestock, all of which had been rudely disturbed from their favorite haunts in the trees, and had plunged down into the depths of an umbrella. With this large assortment safely in its folds, we carried the umbrella home in the manner most people carry an umbrella, using it as a walking stick. Every now and again we would give it a jolt on the ground to deter even the boldest beetle from climbing up the inside. We were in Florida at

the time, and tropical thunderstorms sometimes
happen very quickly there. One moment the sun is
shining brilliantly; the next, the heavens open up and
a deluge descends. We were just about half-way home
when the thunderstorm happened. Down came the
rain, up went the umbrella—and down came a multi-
tude of creatures upon our heads! It rained beetles and
spiders and bugs and caterpillars and Uncle Tom
Cobley and all.

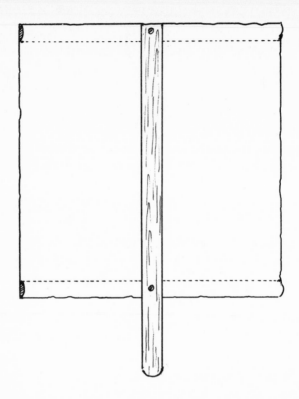

If you prefer not to use a sheet or umbrella, and don't want to run to the expense of a Bignell beating tray, it is not too difficult to make something similar that would serve the same purpose. First of all, obtain a piece of suitable material; strong white canvas is very satisfactory, and it should be about three feet square. Along two opposite edges you will have to make a hem wide enough to allow strips of wood about one and a half inches wide to slide through, one strip through each hem. The strips should be about the same length as the edge of the material. When this stage of the operation is complete, you will find that you already have the main part of the beating tray, that is to say the tray itself. All you need then is something to keep it rigid, and something to serve as a handle, and both jobs can be done by one more strip of wood. This third strip should be a little longer than the other two, and slightly wider; three and a half feet by two inches would be just about right. You attach it by means of screws across the other two strips, one end of it projecting beyond the edge. This strip will serve to keep the whole tray rigid, and the extra few inches projecting beyond the edge will make a handle, as shown in the drawing.

If you use nails instead of screws, the beating tray remains more or less a fixture, and you will have difficulty in getting on a crowded bus with it. If you use screws, however, it can easily be taken apart, rolled up, and tucked under your arm. This do-it-yourself beating tray, simple as it is, should prove very satisfactory and give you a lot of fun. Furthermore, you can name it after yourself.

21: ♊ Containers

Whether you intend collecting insects or reptiles, or both, one thing is certain; you will need boxes. You will obviously have to include in your equipment a number of boxes into which you put any creatures you manage to capture. In this connection, several questions arise. How many boxes to take? What size and shape should they be? What is the best kind to take?

The number of boxes you take with you depends on how many you can carry, whether you are going on a collecting trip alone or with friends, and whether your trip will take up one afternoon or several days. If you are going by yourself for an afternoon or perhaps for a whole day, you would probably be able to manage ten or twelve boxes. If a friend accompanies you—and it is generally more fun to go with others—

you will of course be able to cope with more. On the other hand you may intend doing some collecting while you are away on holiday, over a period of several days. In this case you will have to consider the amount of room you are going to have in your luggage, especially on the journey back home. On the outward journey all your boxes and containers will be empty; you will be able to pack one inside another, and save a lot of room that way, or pack your vests and pants and socks in the boxes. But on your return trip it will be a different story, assuming you have been successful with your collecting and have a good haul to bring back with you. Your containers will be occupied; you will not be able to stuff your pants in with the beetles, or your pajamas with the frogs. In other words you will have to bear in mind the fact that your boxes will take up a comparatively small space on the outward journey but will need much more room on the return trip.

When we go on our collecting trips abroad we take with us a minimum of clothing and a maximum of plastic containers, usually about sixty or seventy. They just about fill up four canvas traveling bags, the sort with zipper fasteners, which we can manage quite happily between us. As we travel by air, the question of weight is very important, and it is something you too will have to consider if you travel by air. On board a plane passengers are normally expected to carry as little as possible, not much more than one small suit-case or an overnight bag being considered enough for most people. We like to carry all our livestock with us, however, which means taking on board all four rather bulging traveling bags and tucking them away under our seats and between our legs. It makes the journey a shade less comfortable for us, but considerably more comfortable for our animals which would otherwise be stowed away in the hold, not to mention being thrown around in the way so many articles of luggage are thrown around. It is most important that you carry your livestock with you; only by doing so can you be sure that they won't be dropped, jerked, bumped, or hurled all over the place.

The size and shape of your boxes is something else to be considered. There is an endless variety, but we seldom have any use for anything smaller than a matchbox, or larger than a cake tin. Some sizes and shapes we have generally found to be suitable for certain creatures. For example, small flat boxes do very well for beetles; small upright ones serve nicely for spiders; long deep ones are just right for lizards. But there is no hard and fast rule about it; you simply use whichever container you think is the most convenient. Those fairly large plastic boxes, originally designed to hold sandwiches for about six people, will be found equally satisfactory for about six small lizards, or a snake, or several grasshoppers, or a whole assortment of beetles, especially if there is still a lingering whiff of an egg-and-tomato sandwich. So with regard to the size and shape of your boxes, the choice is wide open. Take with you several sizes and several shapes, and use the one most suitable for your reptile or insect as you catch it.

Then there is the question of the best type of container to take. Should it be made of glass, wood, metal, plastic, cardboard, cloth, or any other material? From our own experiences we have found plastic containers to be ideal for collecting purposes. They can be easily

obtained from hardware shops and grocery stores; they
come in very many different sizes and shapes; they are
very light in weight, can be quickly and easily cleaned,
and will hold water if necessary. They can also be
peered into without disturbing the occupants, and you
can keep an eye on your livestock and make sure they
are behaving themselves. You may want to show anything particularly interesting or gruesome that you have
caught to some of your friends, and if it is in a plastic
box you can show it around without having to take off
the lid.

Some of the circular plastic boxes have screw-
top lids, which is a desirable feature from the point of
view of security. Others have soft plastic lids which
can be turned up one corner at a time; very useful for
popping in several beetles, one at a time, without the
risk of one popping out as another pops in. All the
lids of all the boxes can be made more secure by the
use of tape, or strong rubber bands. One small draw-
back with some of the plastic boxes is the lack of
ventilation, but this can easily be overcome by piercing
holes through the lids. A sharp point will be necessary
for this. As a matter of fact some creatures, spiders and
centipedes for example, will live very happily without
ventilation.

Generally speaking, then, plastic boxes have many
highly desirable features. Most of our captive insects
and reptiles have lived in them and traveled in them
and have arrived safely in them at the London Zoo. But
there are other kinds of containers which have been
designed specially for certain purposes, and which will
be found very useful. Circular pocket collecting-tins
with perforated tops and an aperture in the side are

well worth taking on your collecting trips. The hole in the side can be opened and closed simply by twisting the outside of the tin, and the idea is that when you have caught an insect, you pop it through the hole and give the outside a twist. The insect is safe inside and you have not had to take the top off at all. You can repeat the operation with more insects as you catch them, and you can push in a morsel of food in the same way with little chance of anything creeping out. Only when you need to take your creatures out will it be necessary to take off the lid.

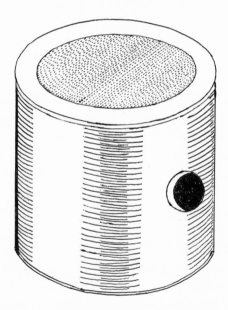

Another very useful type of container is the round cardboard box with a circular piece of glass or plastic at one end. The idea here is that the glass lets in light, and any insect inside this kind of box will be attracted to that end, especially if that end is turned uppermost.

Meanwhile you can remove the other end of the box and put in another insect, which will immediately join its companion doing its level best to find a way out through the glass.

A very different kind of container with a rather specialized use is the test tube. Cigars are sometimes displayed in glass or plastic tubes; toothbrushes often come in a plastic tube too; these would serve the purpose just as well as test tubes. The whole thing is turned into what might be called a block of flats for spiders. When you have found a spider, you place it gently in the tube and encourage it to move right down to the bottom. This you do by carefully and slowly pushing in a plug of cotton wool behind the spider; then push the plug down nearly to the bottom, leaving a little space at the end in which the spider can move around and inspect its new quarters. You then continue your search and no doubt will soon come across another spider. It too is coaxed down into the tube as far as the first plug of cotton wool, and a second plug follows it down. A third spider and a third plug of cotton wool, and a fourth, perhaps even a fifth, depending on the length of the tube, will fill it to capacity.

This block of flats, each floor occupied by a spider, will easily slip into a pocket, and the occupants will survive for several hours without any attention at all. Half a dozen plastic tubes take up very little space, yet will hold twenty or thirty spiders. This avoids the necessity of taking twenty or thirty small plastic boxes, for each spider needs a separate compartment. If two spiders are placed together in one compartment, you are likely to finish up with one rather well-fed specimen.

Cloth bags make very suitable containers for snakes, lizards, frogs, toads, newts and salamanders, and the like. We have found that snakes especially do very well in cloth bags; they simply curl up in the bottom and go to sleep. Ventilation is no problem as air penetrates through the cloth. Food is no problem either; you just don't feed them. Snakes can go for long periods without food; so once the snake is safely inside the bag, the top can be securely fastened and the whole thing hung on a hook in a cupboard out of harm's way. But don't forget all about it and leave it there! Incidentally, the bag should be dampened daily by splashing water over it.

22: The Rest of the Equipment

There are several more items of equipment which serve useful purposes in the collecting of insects and reptiles, though you will probably manage very well without some of them. It depends to some extent on whether you intend to travel about the countryside with nets and boxes and sieves and traps and an assortment of other objects dangling about your person, or whether you intend to travel light, taking only the smallest amount of equipment you consider necessary. Containers you must have; a water net is essential if you intend delving into a pond or stream; the rest of the equipment you decide to take is up to you.

A sieve can be useful, especially near the banks of a river. All sorts of refuse is thrown up on the banks, and beetles especially seem to enjoy it and will frequently be found there. Flood refuse particularly will yield a

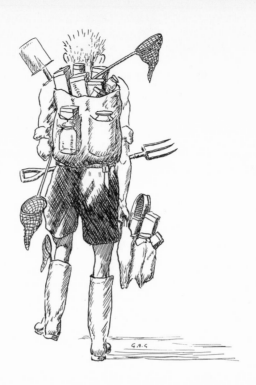

rich haul. If the refuse is floating on the surface of the water you will have to gather it up with a net and place it in the sieve. Shake it and joggle it about in the sieve until the sand and mud have disappeared through the mesh, and then search among the remaining leaves and twigs and other debris for anything that creeps and crawls. It is quite surprising the number of creatures that may be caught in this way. Many of them no doubt will be too small and insignificant for presentation to a zoo, but they will add interest and attractiveness to your own aquarium, or serve as tasty morsels for your goldfish.

It is quite a simple matter to make your own sieve. You need a round shallow cake tin or biscuit tin or toffee tin; cut out the bottom, and what is left becomes the framework of your sieve. A piece of wire gauze or perforated zinc attached to the frame will complete it. It's as easy as that. You will have to decide on the mesh, of course; three or four to the inch for quite large insects, or ten to the inch for smaller ones would probably be adequate. The sieve should be fairly shallow, though not so shallow that the contents will be flung over the sides when it is shaken. A cover will help to prevent this, and the lid will serve perfectly as the cover. If your do-it-yourself sieve is too deep, it becomes rather a bulky object to carry. You want to avoid carrying too many bulky objects on your collecting trips, especially if you do some of your traveling by public transportation. You just can't go jabbing people in the ribs with a sieve.

A sieve can be useful too for sifting loose soil collected with the aid of a trowel or small spade or fork. If by any chance you are spending a holiday on a farm, try and persuade the farmer to plow a field while you are there. If he can manage this, walk behind the plow as he is doing it. All sorts of insects will come to light in the general disturbance caused by the upheaval of the soil, but they will quickly burrow back into the ground. With a sieve in one hand and a trowel in the other, scoop them up quickly and dump them in the sieve. Any loose soil will fall through, and when you have a collection of creatures falling over each other in the sieve, transfer them to containers. You will be kept pretty well occupied digging away at the overturned clods of earth, and your collection of beetles and other creatures will grow enormously, especially if you are nimble.

A small hand-trowel, incidentally, is a very handy tool to have, not only for collecting soil for sifting, but also for digging into any patch of ground, turning over dead leaves and debris, poking among the under-growth, levering up pieces of bark from trees, and for many other purposes.

A good strong knife or a stout screwdriver can also be used to lever up the bark from trees, or to dislodge a beetle or spider that has taken shelter in a crack. A pair of forceps or tweezers will also serve to remove crack-loving creatures. Be careful not to push them farther in, though, or squash them flat.

Traps of one sort or another are used by expert ento-mologists, and are often quite complicated and expensive pieces of equipment. However, if you intend staying in one district for any length of time, you will find that a simple homemade trap will save you a lot of time in your search for insects. Broadly speaking, traps are of two kinds: those that lure by light, and those that lure by smell.

A perfectly ordinary trap that lures by light, one that does not even have to be made, is a lighted room at night with the windows wide open. Moths and other insects will come floating in through the windows. Lamp posts too will attract a great number of insects, especially in tropical countries. For that matter any light will attract some insects; the great thing is to devise an efficient means of trapping them. One method is to place a bowl or bucket of water below the electric-light bulb in a room. Insects that have flown into the room, attracted first by light, will hover around the bulb; then they will see it reflected in the water below and will be attracted by that, promptly flying straight down into it. Naturally, you have to be present all the time with a small net or a pair of forceps to rescue the poor, wet, soggy little things; or else cover the bowl with some sort of wire screen or a sheet of glass, and pick them up from that. In some countries enormous numbers of insects are trapped in this way, especially moths. More than once we have sat down to dinner after an exhausting day, and ordered soup. We both happen to have a particular liking for soup. Then, after an agonizing wait, in comes the soup, and in pops a moth. Then a second, and a third, and a whole succession of moths plunge in before

we have had time to pick up a spoon. Pea soup becomes moth soup. The answer, of course, is to remove yourself and your dinner to a dark corner where there are no lights to attract the moths. The only trouble is that you might find yourself about to eat a frog instead of a moth. Still, if you are keen you will add the frog to your collection.

A white surface such as a sheet suspended close to a light will also attract a great number of insects. They will usually flutter around the light for a short period and then settle on the sheet. All you have to do then is simply remove them by holding a jar or other suitable container over the insects, and knock them in with the lid. An apparatus of this kind is very easy to set up. You need a piece of white cloth about five or six feet square, or a sheet; a length of cord, or some stout string; and a pole or strip of wood about six feet long. Tie the pole horizontally to two convenient objects such as branches at the position selected for the trap. The middle of a garden might be a good spot. Then suspend the sheet from the pole, allowing a narrow strip to lie flat on the ground. Finally place a strong light just in front of the sheet; a powerful flashlight would do, especially if the bulb is visible from the sides, though an electric light would be better. The only other piece of equipment you then require is a chair in which to sit back and wait. Unfortunately in this country there are not many species of beetles that are attracted to light, but in warm climates with night temperatures above 70 degrees Fahrenheit, or 21 degrees Centigrade, success is pretty well guaranteed, particularly if the night is humid.

The other form of trapping, luring by smell, involves

using something left over from lunch: a bit of meat, or
the remains of a kipper, a banana skin, an overripe
plum, or the slice of bread and jam which fell on the
floor and which you were unable to pick up quickly
enough without anyone noticing. Anything of this
nature will serve to lure hungry insects. One method is
simply to place the bait inside a jam jar, bury the jar
in the ground up to the rim, and inspect it from time to
time. You may cover it with a piece of bark or a flat
stone to keep out the rain, but make sure that you do
not cover it so thoroughly that you keep out the insects
as well. A more refined method is to place a funnel in
the mouth of the jar, and attach a piece of cotton or
string across the top of the funnel. From the middle of
this piece of cotton suspend another length, at the end
of which you tie your plum or other piece of bait. And

there it dangles, temptingly, near the bottom of the funnel but without touching the sides of it. The whole lot is buried in the ground up to the level of the top of the funnel, and covered to keep out the rain. Unwary but hungry insects will approach, hover on the brink, wave their antennae, and, in their efforts to reach the appetizing delicacy, will slither down the side of the funnel and into the jar. If you feel very kindhearted you could place a small fragment of something tasty inside the jar to comfort them.

Trapping by light or smell is a satisfactory and rather lazy way of catching insects. It requires very little energy on your part, and has none of the thrill of the chase. Nevertheless, with a trap you may lure some night-flying creatures you might otherwise never see. You will certainly capture varieties which you would never capture by day. Incidentally, while on the subject of traps, it is quite a good plan to set up an ordinary flytrap, not because you will want to add any flies to

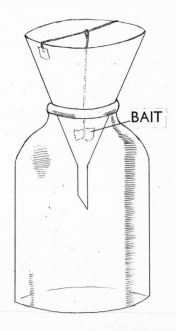

BAIT

your collection, but any you do catch will do very nicely for lunch for any spiders you may have in your containers. There is nothing a spider likes more than a nice fat, juicy common or garden housefly; lizards, chameleons, geckos, frogs and toads find them very tasty too.

A few other items of equipment remain to be mentioned: a haversack or bag in which to carry all your boxes, a notebook in which to record dates and places and other information you want to remember, a reference book from which to identify species captured, and a pair of gloves. We have always found stout gloves or gauntlets a great help. When we are turning over logs, lifting boulders, searching through the undergrowth, and pulling loose bark from the trees, there is always a chance of disturbing a scorpion or a poisonous spider or snake, or something else that will object to being disturbed, quite naturally, and will show its objection by biting or stinging. Very many of our captured creatures have been found lurking underneath a log or rock, and when lifting it we have had to grasp it firmly underneath, thereby giving the creature a glorious opportunity to jab at a finger with all its might. Wearing gloves will give a certain measure of protection.

23: Hide and Seek

Many insects hide. They hide in flowers and they hide in bushes; they hide in tufts of grass, under clods of earth, in among damp leaves; under stones and logs and rocks and fallen trees; in the compost heap and down in the manure heap; in moss, under the bark of trees; in old ruins, in cracks in walls, under tiles and slates; in shallow water where there is plenty of vegetation, under the rocks on a river bed, or at the bottom of a pond. Anywhere. Indoors or out of doors, daytime or nighttime, rain or shine, insects go about their business, eating and getting eaten, living and dying as Nature intended. Spiders also spend much of their time hidden away in rather the same sort of places. Small reptiles do so, too. Some of the smaller lizards love to scamper about under the carpet of dead leaves in the forest, or in and out among the broken rocks and bricks of a ruined building.

In many tropical and semitropical countries, geckos hide behind the pictures hanging on the wall or at the back of the sideboard. Then in the evening, when moths and other insects are attracted by the lights, the geckos will come out of hiding and stalk them, creeping up slowly until within snapping distance. Then snap! and a moth disappears down a mouth. Occasionally a gecko may lose its foothold in its excitement and fall down somebody's neck, or land on the cat, or in the milk jug. Throughout the night they snap up the moths and insects that settle on the walls or the ceilings, but by morning there is not a gecko to be seen. They have all retired to their hiding places behind the pictures. Snakes, too, will hide under boulders, in holes in the ground, or in the hollows of dead trees, and among the bracken and vegetation on waste ground; sometimes they will hide near streams and ponds and open stretches of water, often right in the water among the reeds.

Reptiles, then, as well as insects, spend a lot of time hiding. You, then, must spend a lot of time seeking. If it is your aim to make a collection of reptiles and insects, you will have to seek them out; they won't come to you. It is worth remembering that they are cold-blooded creatures; their body temperature varies according to the temperature of the surrounding air. We humans are warm-blooded, and so are all other mammals and birds. Our body temperature remains more or less the same whether we are sun-bathing on a tropical beach or playing snakes and ladders in an igloo. In warm weather, therefore, when the temperature is somewhere around 70 or 80 degrees, insects and reptiles are likely to be much more active and therefore much more visible. If, however, the temperature goes soaring up beyond 90 degrees or into the hundreds, then most creatures will very sensibly seek a cool shady spot in which to shelter and rest. We do precisely the same.

It follows, then, that a collecting expedition in a temperate climate will be far more successful in summer than it would in the depths of winter, though the first really warm day of spring often brings out all manner of creatures. Seek, and you shall find. Search in all the likely places mentioned in this chapter, and a few unlikely places as well. Of course, a lot depends on where you live. If, for instance, you live in the heart of New York, Minneapolis, or Seattle, you will not expect to find very much; if, on the other hand, you live on the outskirts of these cities or somewhere down in the South, you never know what might turn up in your garden. As already mentioned in a previous chapter, we found a lot of highly interesting creatures in and around the scented and immaculate gardens of Palm Beach, although the scented and immaculate owners of those gardens were probably unaware of their existence. As a general rule, the warmer your climate, the greater your variety of creepy crawlies.

In the United States as a whole, there are rather more than a hundred varieties of snakes and rather less than a hundred varieties of lizards, as well as a pleasing assortment of turtles, frogs, toads, newts and salamanders. Most varieties are to be found in the southern States, with the selection becoming more and more scarce as one proceeds north in the general direction of Canada. But even in the most northerly States and in Canada itself, quite a lot of reptiles can be found by the really determined collector—certainly more than exist in most of Europe. England, for instance, has only three kinds of snakes, three lizards, three newts, three frogs and two toads—no turtles at all. A rather wider assortment can be found in southern Europe, in countries bordering the Mediterranean, and still more in the countries of north Africa.

No cobras inhabit the United States, but rattlesnakes do; there are several varieties of rattlesnakes, some of which are to be found in most States and all of which should be regarded with the deepest respect. Indeed, they should be left severely alone except by the most ardent collector. Fortunately, rattlesnakes generally give you some warning of their presence; they rattle. And when they rattle, you, if you are wise, should take heed and depart—unless you are an ardent snake-collector.

Much the same warning applies to coral snakes, copperheads and water moccasins, none of which rattle but all of which can be exceedingly uncivil if you start probing into their private affairs. The coral snake happens to be one of the world's most vividly colored snakes as well as exceedingly dangerous; but as it is rather shy and spends most of the day underground, coming out only at night to feed, comparatively few people have ever come across one. Probably even fewer people ever wish to come across one—except, of course, the very ardent. By now, the reader may have reached the conclusion that we are among the very ardent; and the reader will be very correct. We positively yearned to come across a coral snake during our collecting trips in Florida, and did so only once—among the private collection of reptiles belonging to a lady who taught biology. She, too, was among the very ardent, obviously, but was kind enough to let us have her specimen which, in due course, safely arrived at the London Zoo in a plastic box.

The actual capture of a creature, whether it be reptile or insect, depends largely on two things: the creature and you. Sharp eyes are necessary to find the animal, but nimble fingers are equally necessary to catch it. Some insects may be caught with ease; slow-moving beetles or certain spiders practically give themselves up. On the other hand, most lizards will disappear as fast as their legs will carry them, certainly faster than your legs will carry you when you attempt to catch up with them. However, a certain amount of practice and a fair amount of luck will yield results in time. So will the native population, if you make it worth their while. On our trips to Morocco we invariably found that all the small boys and teenagers were far more adept at diving into prickly clumps of cactus than we were, and nearly always caught the lizard which had scuttled there for protection. Many of the children were only too delighted to join in the fun and several of them who came out with us regularly and knew just what we wanted were rewarded with various trinkets and oddments. The older ones were very happy to receive articles of clothing, and quite a selection of our shirts, shoes and socks have finished up in the proud possession of these Arab children, to be worn only on Sundays.

A word or two of advice is necessary here in connection with the business of catching lizards. Certain varieties possess a tail which is not a permanent fixture; catch a lizard by its tail and you may see the lizard dashing off at top speed, leaving you still holding the tail. It can wriggle out of trouble by wriggling out of its tail, so to speak. Since it is highly unlikely that you want just a tail to present to the zoo, you must make sure that you grab your lizard firmly around its body; the chances are that it will remain in one piece.

Sometimes lizards may be caught by quickly placing a suitable plastic box over them, and then carefully sliding a flat sheet of metal or cardboard underneath. The whole thing can then be turned right side up, when the lizard will fall to the bottom of the box and the cardboard can be replaced by the lid. Lizards can move extremely fast, however, so care must be taken not to damage the creature by trapping a leg or a toe and squashing it; care is just as important as speed.

Many insects can be caught in a similar manner. Scorpions are comparatively easy to scoop up into a box, and if the box is a fairly deep one, they will have difficulty in climbing up the sides. A certain amount of soil or leaves may be scooped up with the scorpion; so much the better, for it will feel just that much more at home if a fragment of its native habitat goes along with it.

Certain animals must be kept in solitary confinement. There are cannibals in the insect world, and it is asking for total war to put two of them together. In arithmetic, one plus one equals two, but with certain insects, one plus one means a meal for one—and leaves only one. You will prove it to your sorrow if you put one spider in with another, or one centipede with another. Scorpions are inclined to fancy each other, too, and a Praying Mantis likes nothing better for lunch than a Praying Mantis, even if it's an uncle. So keep your cannibals in separate containers; they can glare at each other through their plastic boxes, and make faces at each other, but at least they won't be able to eat each other.

24: Feeding

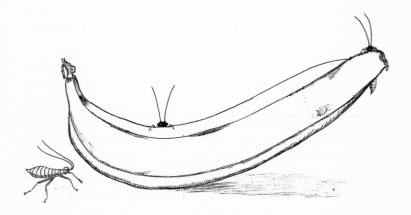

Collecting reptiles and insects is one thing; looking after them is another. Once your creatures have been safely put away in their plastic boxes, the problem of feeding them arises and, in some cases, may require your immediate attention. In the wild state, of course, every living creature has to fend for itself, and a good many animals find themselves suddenly being gobbled up by a good many other animals. Some are purely meat eaters, others prefer a vegetarian diet; quite a number eat both meat and vegetables, while a few are perfectly content to eat each other. In days gone by, it was by no means unknown for man to eat man; even today, in very distant and remote corners of the globe, it is occasionally reported that certain tribes have raided their neighbors, killed a few off, and eaten selected specimens. By and large, however, we consider ourselves highly cultured where food is concerned, and most of us would prefer a slice of roast beef for lunch rather than a slice of roast uncle. Animals, however, are less concerned with forming cultural relations than they are with eating their relations, and in some cases—the Praying Mantis, for instance—a wife will gladly eat her husband without the tiniest tinge of grief.

If, on the other hand, a wild animal finds itself in a cage or a plastic box, it is immediately deprived of its natural ability to hunt food when it feels the need; it may actually have been in the process of hunting when it was captured, in which case it is likely to be hungry right from the start. This, then, is the reason why your immediate attention should be given to the problem of feeding your collection, since a well-fed animal is much more likely to settle down in its plastic box than a hungry one. Fortunately, most animals need only be fed once a day; they are not very fussy about having a lunch hour, or a snack at eleven in the morning, or another snack before going to bed, and there are a good many reptiles and insects which can survive for several days without any food at all.

It has already been mentioned, in an earlier chapter, that if you are enjoying a two-to-three-weeks' holiday abroad and have decided to do some collecting for the Zoo, it is a good plan to leave the actual collecting until the last week, or even the last four or five days. This cuts down the length of time during which you will have to feed your captive creatures; as far as snakes are concerned you won't have to feed them at all for they can manage very comfortably without food for a week or longer. Some snakes actually go without food for several weeks.

Another way to simplify the feeding problem is to release your earlier specimens every time you find a fresh one. If, for example, you are on holiday in Morocco and find a nice, fat, warty Moroccan toad which you consider would make a very acceptable gift for the Zoo, put it safely away in a suitably sized plastic box and keep it out of sight of your mother who will probably shudder at the sight of it. If you should then discover another Moroccan toad two or three days later, let the first one go and keep the second one. If you come across yet a third one, perhaps on the last day of your holiday, keep the new one and let the second one go. This will relieve you of the necessity of spending a good deal of your time searching for the right kind of food; and you can at least be sure of having a freshly caught specimen when you arrive at the Zoo.

On the whole, reptiles and insects are not difficult to feed, and are probably a lot easier than mammals or birds. Some reptiles, as already stated, can manage very well on nothing at all for several days; if snakes are kept in cotton bags as recommended, they will in all probability sleep blissfully until they reach the Zoo and are put on display. Even then they may go to sleep again. Lizards too may go for quite long periods without nourishment, though it is a simple matter to give them a few live insects; moths, grasshoppers, and flies can easily be popped in with the lizards in their plastic boxes, and will keep them amused. Frogs and toads will also feel very happy if live insects or a couple of plump worms are pushed into their containers.

One thing you should bear in mind is that certain species have to be kept in solitary confinement. The Praying Mantis has already been mentioned; spiders must be kept apart too, for they rather enjoy eating up each other; and centipedes should be separated also. All these cannibals are comparatively easy to feed, and they will relish a moth or a fly or meal worm. Some spiders become almost tame, and will delicately accept a fly offered to them on the end of a pair of tweezers. One word of warning is necessary in connection with a particularly spidery spider known as the Bird-eating Spider; don't handle it, and don't feed it. Actually, it is most unlikely that you will ever find one, unless you can afford to take your holidays in South America, but they do occasionally turn up in a bunch of bananas, having managed to stow away in a banana ship. A Bird-eating Spider is easily identified; huge and hairy, it looks rather like a medium-sized rissole with legs, and badly in need of a shave. It is the hairs that will set up an irritation if you should handle one of these creatures.

Beetles give very little trouble as a rule; many species find all the nourishment they require in a slice of apple or orange, or a choice lettuce leaf. If you are uncertain what to give your beetles, try experimenting with several kinds of fruit; bananas often go down well with many beetles. If you have a scorpion or two, they will enjoy a small piece of raw meat, or a meal worm. On most of our collecting trips we have generally found scorpions to be sufficiently plentiful to allow us to replenish our stock from day to day, thus avoiding the necessity of feeding them at all.

For quick and easy reference, we have listed at the end of this chapter some of the more common reptiles, amphibians, and insects which you may be able to capture, and the type of food they require. Included among the insects are several creatures which, scientifically speaking, are not insects at all, but as this is not a scientific book, all such creatures—spiders, scorpions, centipedes, etc.—have been lumped together as insects purely for convenience.

Perhaps more important than food is the question of water. Whereas a good many reptiles can go for long periods without food, they do like a drink of water from time to time, especially if the weather is warm—and most reptiles come from warm climates. It is sometimes enough simply to sprinkle the contents of the containers with fresh water; if the box is furnished with a tuft of grass or a leafy branch, splash that with water. This after all is precisely what happens when it rains. Snakes can be kept damp in their cotton bags by sprinkling the cloth liberally with water. Frogs and toads must be kept in a dampish condition all the time, and the best way to ensure this is to keep a lump of moss soaked in water at one end of the container.

Many of the insects will quench their thirst with the natural fruit juices, but spiders very definitely need water. An easy method of supplying their water is to place a small ball of absorbent cotton in each container, and squirt a few drops of water over it daily with a medicine dropper.

There is one very important point to remember,

especially if you are collecting abroad. NEVER allow your plastic boxes to stand in the sun, unless you want to present the Zoo with some beautifully cooked specimens. It is very easy to keep a beetle or spider in a plastic container, and then place the container on the window sill, or on a table in the corner, forgetting that later in the day the sun may shine right onto and into the container. It would not be very long before your beetle was cooked right through, nicely done on both sides.

Feeding your livestock leads naturally to one more problem: cleaning the containers out. Here again a lot depends on the length of time your animals are likely to remain in their boxes before they reach their final destination. It is always desirable that they should arrive in a presentable condition, and unless their containers are cleaned reasonably often, they will look rather sorry for themselves on arrival. Probably the easiest way to clean out a container is to transfer the occupant into some temporary abode, and then empty the box completely, wash it out thoroughly, and refurnish it with fresh greenery. We have often found that the bathtub makes a most useful temporary abode; the sides are too smooth and steep and slippery for most creatures to climb; and they can stretch their legs and enjoy the comparative freedom of the tub for half an hour or so while their containers are being cleaned and washed. For that matter there is no harm in keeping them in the tub all the time, unless of course somebody wants it for another purpose. As far as we are concerned, bathtubs were invented for lizards and tortoises and frogs and toads.

List of Animals in alphabetical order, and Food Requirements

BEETLES	Apple, orange, banana, lettuce; fruit and vegetables generally
CENTIPEDES	Raw meat
CHAMELEONS	Live food; flies, grasshoppers
CICADAS	Green leaves, grass, green stuff generally
CRICKETS	Green stuff and fruit generally; dock leaves
FROGS	Live food; earthworms, grasshoppers, moths, beetles
GECKOS	Live food; flies, moths, grasshoppers, cockroaches
GRASSHOPPERS	Green stuff generally; dandelions
LIZARDS	Live food; flies, moths, meal worms
LOCUSTS	Grass and leaves
MILLIPEDES	Leaves of privet and forsythia; fruit
MOLE CRICKETS	Vegetables; carrot, swede, potato
NEWTS	Small earthworms and water insects
PRAYING MANTIS	Live food; moths, flies, grasshoppers
SALAMANDERS	Small earthworms and water insects
SCORPIONS	Live food or raw meat; meal worms, grasshoppers
SLOW-WORMS	Live food; meal worms, moths
SNAILS	Fruit generally; banana, apple
SNAKES	Generally, no food required
SPIDERS	Live food; flies, moths
STICK INSECTS	Privet and bramble twigs with plenty of leaves, including rose
TERRAPINS	Insects, worms, grubs, fish
TOADS	Live food; earthworms, moths, beetles
TORTOISES	Fruit and vegetables generally; apple, lettuce

TURTLES	Insects, worms, fish
WATER BEETLES	Small live food or raw meat
WATER SCORPIONS	Small live food or raw meat
WATER SPIDERS	Small live food or raw meat

25: A Word or Two About a Snake or Two

How long is the longest snake in the world? This is one of the questions most frequently asked about snakes, yet nobody has produced a thoroughly satisfactory answer to it. Nobody knows for certain; if there was a positive answer to the question, the authorities and the experts would no longer be involved in endless arguments and speculation concerning the question. But it is the sort of question which is never likely to be answered positively, once and for all, for the simple reason that no one is ever likely to know. The longest snake that has ever been recorded was a Reticulated Python which measured thirty-three feet. But who can say for certain that there isn't a Reticulated Python which measures thirty-four feet? In the Malayan jungle where some of the world's largest snakes are to be found there may well be specimens

even longer still. Colonel Fawcett, who disappeared in
the Brazilian jungle in 1925, was reported to have shot
a giant Anaconda measuring over sixty feet, though
admittedly this was partly guesswork as some of the
snake was lying submerged in water, and the Colonel
had to estimate that bit of its length. He had further
reports of even longer specimens which exceeded eighty
feet in length. Until there is positive and absolute
proof, however, that such gigantic monsters do actually
exist, one has to be content with accepting a mere thirty-
three-foot specimen as being the longest known so far.
Even that is a lot of snake, especially if you want to put
it into a plastic box.

One must bear in mind, too, the difficulties of measuring or even estimating the length of a snake with any
accuracy, especially large ones. Using a ruler is not
going to help much. A tape measure would be more
helpful if the snake was stretched out full length and
fast asleep. But snakes do not normally stretch themselves out at full length before going to sleep; they
coil themselves up, which makes the job of measuring
much harder, if not altogether impossible. If by chance
one happened to come across a dead snake in some
remote jungle, and by another chance happened to be
carrying a tape measure, it might seem to be a good
opportunity to stretch it out and measure it. But how
does one stretch out something that may weigh anything up to two hundred pounds? The authorities and
the experts will simply have to continue with their
arguments and speculations.

The other very popular question continually being
asked about snakes is: Which is the most poisonous
snake in the world? Here again there is no definite,
positive answer. The Tiger Snake of Australia is

thought to have the most concentrated venom of all snakes, but that does not mean that to be bitten by a Tiger Snake is invariably followed by certain death.

All sorts of factors enter into the question of how poisonous a poisonous snake really is. Assuming someone has been bitten by a venomous snake, how much of the poison has actually entered his body? Is he in a good state of health, or is he perhaps elderly and frail? Will he remain quite still after being bitten, or will he go rushing about looking for help? Will he have any idea of the first-aid measures to adopt? Did the snake bite him on a bare hand or leg, or did the fangs first penetrate some article of clothing? All these factors, and others too, have a very definite bearing on whether the victim will recover, so it is impossible to say with absolute certainty that one venomous snake is more dangerous than another. Cobras and kraits probably account for most of the snake deaths in India. Many of the natives walk about in bare feet, so they have no protection whatever should they accidentally tread on a snake. Furthermore, many of them are not permitted to harm any creature on account of their religion, with the result that in some areas snakes flourish, and no action is taken to control their numbers or to eliminate them altogether. To walk about barefooted in such a region is asking for trouble. Another Australian snake, the Taipan, is considered by some to be one of the most deadly of all snakes. Most people living in the bush in Australia are very snake-conscious for the very good reason that poisonous snakes in that country are comparatively common. In most countries harmless snakes outnumber the dangerous ones, but in Australia the proportion of venomous snakes is much greater.

In Africa the Gaboon Viper is one of the most poisonous snakes, as well as one of the most attractive from the
point of view of its coloring and pattern. The Puff
Adder and the Mambas are very dangerous, and one of
the Cobras rejoices in its ability to spit its poison at its
enemies, aiming generally for the eyes. In America
several species of Rattlesnakes, the beautifully colored
Coral Snake, encircled in bands of red, black, and
yellow, and the Cottonmouth, or Water Moccasin, are
all venomous. In England there is only one dangerous
snake, the Adder or Viper, and although death from
snake bite in England is an uncommon occurrence,
nevertheless the Adder is not a snake to take liberties
with. Most of the sea snakes are poisonous, too.

It is difficult, then, to point a finger at any one
particular species and accuse it of being the most
dangerous snake in the world. Even the mildly poisonous ones can be potentially lethal, and it is wise to
consider *all* venomous snakes as dangerous. Later in
this chapter we will go into the question of first-aid
measures that can be taken in the event of snake bite.

It is interesting to note that venomous snakes do not
attain the extraordinary lengths of some of the non-
venomous species. The longest poisonous snake on
record was a Hamadryad Cobra which measured
eighteen feet two inches, though it is very exceptional
to find one as long as that. So that is a comfort. Slightly
less comforting, however, and something well worth
remembering, is the fact that a six-inch poisonous
snake can be every bit as dangerous as a six-yard specimen. A newly born snake can kill with its first bite just
as effectively as a much older snake with years of biting
experience.

It is extraordinary how so many normally intelligent people shudder at the mention of snakes, and turn pale at the very idea of handling one. There is a general tendency to regard them as slimy creatures, though in truth they are very definitely not slimy. Most people express surprise when they handle a snake for the first time and feel how dry it is. A few species are actually rough to the touch, but most of them give an impression of dryness. Naturally a snake will appear to be slimy when it emerges from water, or after moving about in wet grass. Certainly a snake will wriggle and squirm in an effort to escape if it is picked up. And sometimes the scales covering their bodies may reflect light and give the appearance of being smooth and slimy. But hold one firmly in the hand and you will realize that far from being slimy it is dry and not at all unpleasant to touch.

Many weird and wonderful stories have been told about snakes, and it is incredible that some of the most unlikely and imaginative stories are widely believed by civilized men and women. A fairly common American snake is known as a Milk Snake, and there are people who actually believe that it takes up residence on a farm and goes around milking the cows. That it takes up residence on a farm may be perfectly true, and no doubt it will enjoy drinking the milk put out for the cat, but surely no one in his right senses will believe that it has learned to milk the cow as well. If they believe such nonsense as that, they might just as well believe that another American snake called the King Snake goes around wearing a crown or that the Garter Snake wears garters.

Another fallacy widely accepted is that a mother

snake will swallow her young for protection. If a snake swallows another snake it is not for protection; it is for lunch. Of course it is perfectly true that some people have seen a snake disappearing inside another one's mouth, and yet they accept the very unlikely explanation that it is offering protection, instead of the perfectly natural explanation that it is having a meal. Rather than be convinced that the snake is behaving quite naturally, these people prefer to believe in strange and impossible happenings.

` Another false yet widespread belief is that snakes have the power of hypnotizing their prey. This belief may have its origin in the fact that some small creatures become so frightened when they find themselves confronted by a snake that they are rendered quite incapable of moving until it is too late. Even we human beings sometimes find ourselves "struck dumb with terror" when frightened suddenly and unexpectedly. This is not the same thing as being hypnotized, however, and when a small animal finds itself in the presence of a snake, it too is probably "struck dumb with terror" and becomes a meal.

A great many people believe that a snake's tongue is poisonous. Even though it may be forked, it is most certainly not poisonous. A snake's tongue is completely harmless, and is in fact a well-developed sense organ, used partly as an aid in smelling and partly as a means of feeling. A snake is not equipped with hands and fingers with which to feel, so its tongue makes up for this by taking over the sense of touch. It darts in and out fairly frequently, particularly when the snake is suspicious, or shows an interest in something. Even a poisonous snake cannot possibly poison with its tongue.

Snake charmers delight in making you believe that they possess a certain strange power over their snakes, and that one of their magical powers is to make the snake sway from side to side to the sound of music. The snake charmer will sit cross-legged in front of his snake, and will start blowing on some musical instrument, swaying from side to side as he does so. Thereupon the snake will rear its head up and start swaying too. This performance will impress the onlooker; he will marvel at the snake's ability to dance, and will come to the conclusion that the snake is not only thoroughly enjoying itself but that it positively adores music. The onlooker would be wrong, however. Snakes are deaf. The snake charmer can puff and blow till he is purple in the face, but it will have no effect whatever on the snake. It is his movement that matters, the side-

G.A.G.

to-side swaying of the snake charmer that the reptile follows by swaying too. The music itself is of no importance; it matters not whether he puffs out a Beethoven symphony or blows out the latest pop record. Provided he sways as he plays, the snake will sway too, and the onlooker will gaze in wonder and admiration, and ponder over the magic and mystery of it all.

Some people believe that certain snakes propel themselves along by placing their tails in their mouths, thereby forming a loop, and then rolling across the countryside in the manner of a hoop. It is hard to imagine how such stories originate, and harder still to realize that people have faith in them and believe them to be true. Fortunately there is little or no harm in believing fairy tales.

The chances of being bitten by a venomous snake in Great Britain are slim; the chances of being knocked down by a car are far greater. The only poisonous snake in England is the Adder, sometimes known as the Viper, and it can generally be recognized by the zigzag pattern along its back, though this is sometimes broken up into blotches rather than a clearly defined zigzag. The color of the Adder varies; it may be different shades of brown or gray, or a dirty yellow, or even black, or a combination of some of these colors. It is not a rare snake; in fact it is quite plentiful in certain areas, especially in the spring when it may be seen enjoying the warmth of the sunshine after its winter hibernation.

Abroad, especially in the tropics and semitropical countries, there are of course many more species of poisonous snakes, though the chances of being bitten by one of them are still slim, unless you are foolish and walk about in bare feet. There is no certain way of telling whether a snake is poisonous or not. Many snakes with heads shaped like triangles are very poisonous indeed, but there are many snakes with quite slender heads which are equally poisonous. Perhaps the only reasonably sure way of determining whether a snake is venomous or not is to open its mouth and peer inside; if it has fangs, it is poisonous. It is a method we do not recommend, however. Unless you are something of an expert and can identify a snake without the slightest shadow of doubt, it is wise to treat every snake with the utmost caution. Even non-venomous snakes can bite.

So we come now to the first-aid treatment for snake bite. There is no reason why anyone should remain in complete ignorance about the immediate steps to be taken in the unlikely event of snake bite. To know what to do is halfway to being successful when doing it. You may be out with a party of friends on a country ramble, and one of the party gets bitten by a snake; if you are the only member of the party with some knowledge of first aid, you may be instrumental in saving his life by your prompt treatment.

Let us assume, then, that you are in the country with your friends, and one of them does get bitten on the back of the hand. Now the first thing to remember is to keep calm. The patient especially must keep absolutely calm, and you can help him a great deal by keeping calm yourself. It is imperative that the victim must not exert himself unnecessarily. The more he moves about, the more the poison will move about, and that is precisely what you must try to avoid. Your first action then, after quieting the patient, will be to prevent the poison from traveling up his arm by tying something fairly tightly around his arm, above the elbow. You can use a handkerchief, or a tie, or even a shoelace. This is known as applying a tourniquet. One important thing to remember in connection with a tourniquet is that it must be loosened every quarter of an hour for about half a minute. Action number one then is to keep the patient calm and apply a tourniquet.

Action number two will be to cut the wound. This may sound somewhat alarming, but upon reflection it will be realized that it is really a perfectly sane and sensible thing to do. A certain amount of poison has entered the body, so the obvious thing to do is to get rid of the poison as quickly as possible. This is best done by cutting the wound and causing it to bleed more freely; the blood flowing out will probably take some of the poison with it. It is possible that there will be two marks where the fangs penetrated the skin, and the hand will have swollen to some extent. Cutting it, therefore, may not be as painful as one would expect, for you will be cutting into the swelling. It is advisable to make a small cut over each fang mark, about a quarter of an inch long and a quarter of an inch deep, which will increase the flow of blood and allow some of the poison to flow out with it.

Action number three will be to extract more poison still by sucking it out. This, too, may sound alarming, but there is no risk at all provided your lips are not cracked or cut in any way. For that matter there is no reason why the patient himself should not suck out the poison, assuming of course that he is able to; if he was bitten on the heel or the sole of his foot, he would have to be something of a contortionist to reach it with his mouth. (In America, where there are more poisonous snakes than there are in Great Britain, it is possible to buy a special instrument for sucking out poison from a wound.)

While all this is going on, another member of the party will have gone off in search of a telephone to call an ambulance; or he will have endeavored to find a local doctor and bring him to the scene. Your promptness in rendering first aid is certainly of the utmost importance, but it is only first aid; expert care and attention as soon as possible are also vitally necessary. So get help quickly; in fact one of the very first things to do is to send for help. This could well be included in action number one, provided there is a third member of the party. If, however, the party consisted only of yourself and the victim, and you are in a fairly remote area, finding help might take a considerable time, and it would be wiser to render first-aid treatment before going off to look for help. Help is generally forthcoming even in remote areas.

To sum up, the important things to remember are to keep calm, to apply first aid, and to summon help as soon as possible. With a combination of all three the victim stands a very good chance of making a perfectly sound recovery. It is quite possible that he will be able to help himself by cutting the wound and sucking out the poison; it is possible, on the other hand, that you may have nothing suitable with which to make a cut or for some reason not be able to apply a tourniquet. Perhaps the victim was bitten on the back of his neck. All sorts of things are possible. It is even possible that

the snake was not a poisonous one after all! Nevertheless, it is a good thing to be prepared, and to know
what action to take should the occasion ever arise. It is
worth repeating that to know what to do is halfway to
being successful when doing it.

Acknowledgments

We end this book by thanking those who suggested we should start it, and those who encouraged and helped us in a variety of ways. We are especially grateful to:

Mr. Charles P. Parsons ("Craven Hill"), Zoo Correspondent of the *Evening Standard* and other journals, who started the ball rolling by writing an article in a newspaper about our travels.

Mr. Colin Franklin, who read this article and suggested we should write a book about our collecting trips.

Mr. George Gammon, official artist at the London Zoo, who agreed to do most of the illustrations.

Mr. Clement Newman, who heard all about it and gave us some technical advice.

Mr. George Ashby, Overseer of the Insect House, for reading and correcting the chapters dealing with insects.

Mr. Reginald Lanworn, for doing precisely the same with the reptile chapters.

Mr. Robert Humphrys, for aiding and abetting Mr. Ashby.

Mr. David Ball, for aiding and abetting Mr. Lanworn.

Mr. Roger Dennison, and his children, Scott, Todd, and Lisa, for their interest, encouragement, and advice.

Brian Stewart, Barry Clive, John Clive, Ian Green, Martin Orloff, Gary Castle, Simon Somers, Clive Henry, and David Baker, and the boys of Hereward

House School, Hampstead, who listened to several chapters during their English lessons, helped with some of the photographs, and rendered much valuable assistance.

Mrs. Joyce Dix, and students in her biology class at Riviera Beach High School, Florida, for helping in the collection of specimens.

Mr. John Yealland, Curator of Birds, London Zoo, for looking after one Moorish Magpie, and helping to cope with one female Black Widow.

Mr. Ian Schalburg, Hill Brow School, Somerset, who also helped in the collection of reptiles and insects.

Mr. and Mrs. Ira Dennison of Lake George, N.Y., and Mr. and Mrs. John Ogden of Palm Beach, Florida, for being our relations, and for relinquishing a spare bathroom for our livestock.

Zan, Bruce, and Duane Ricketson, and Michael Eggleston, who guided us to the haunts of all the best snakes around Warrensburg, N.Y.

Jonathan, Timothy, and Thomas Ward, together with James Comstock, who did the same around South Glens Falls, N.Y., and who warned us just in time about the perils of poison ivy.

Irene Clarke, Ivor Cook, David Krouse, and John Stevens, who prodded us at frequent intervals until the book was finished.

Members of the XYZ Club, London Zoo, for providing many specimens for the Zoo, and the material for Chapter 18.